GREAT MINDS ON SMALL THINGS

GREAT MINDS ON SMALL THINGS

The Philosophers' Guide to Everyday Life

Matthew Qvortrup
Illustrated by Taaryn Brench

First published in the United Kingdom by Duckworth in 2023

Duckworth, an imprint of Duckworth Books Ltd
1 Golden Court, Richmond, TW9 1EU, United Kingdom
www.duckworthbooks.co.uk

For bulk and special sales please contact info@duckworthbooks.com

Portions of this work appeared, sometimes in different form, as columns in *Philosophy Now*. Columns include: *Philosophers on Food* (Issue 141: December 2020/January 2021); *Philosophers on Buildings* (Issue 142: February/March 2021); *Philosophers on Hope* (Issue 143: April/May 2021); *Philosophers on Sleeping* (Issue 144: June/July 2021); *Philosophers on Listening* (Issue 145: August/September 2021); *Philosophers on Marriage* (Issue 146: October/November 2021); *Philosophers on Laughter* (Issue 147: December 2021/January 2022); *Philsophers on Play* (Issue 148: February/March 2022); *Philosophers on War & Peace* (Issue 149: April/May 2022); *Philosophers on Wine* (Issue 150: June/July 2022); *Philosophers on Coffee* (Issue 151: August/September 2022).

A CIP catalogue record for this book is available from the British Library.

Typesetting and design by Danny Lyle

Printed and bound in Great Britain by Clays

1 3 5 7 9 10 8 6 4 2

Hardback ISBN: 978-0-71565-4-965
eISBN: 978-0-71565-4-972

I am grateful to Rick Lewis and Grant Bartley from *Philosophy Now* for letting me write for them – and for letting me rework material that I first tried out on their readers. I am grateful to Rowan Cope, my editor at Duckworth, and to my tireless agent, Jon Curzon, whose indefatigable support and suggestions helped in the early stages of this book. Lastly, I am grateful to the staff and colleagues of the Australian National University College of Law who hosted me and endured the babbles of this writer during the undertaking of this pointless – and hence valuable – endeavour.

This book is dedicated to all
frivolous philosophical minds

FOREWORD

In 1978, the new-wave band Talking Heads released an album entitled *More Songs About Buildings and Food* – that is, the kinds of things international rock stars normally *don't* sing about. Pop and rock songs are usually variations on the theme of love – tracks like Rose Royce's 1976 hit 'Car Wash' and George Harrison's 'Taxman' – written in response to a marginal tax rate of ninety-six per cent! – are among the rare exceptions.

Philosophers, likewise, have a narrow focus on epistemology,* metaphysics,* ethics,* logic* and trifles like the meaning of life. But, just occasionally, the great minds stray from their usual turf and write about, for example, vegetables (Ludwig Wittgenstein), buildings (Martin Heidegger), food (Thomas Hobbes), wine (John Locke) and faeces (Plato), to name but a few. This book brings together – for your edification and, I hope, entertainment – the musings of our great minds on life's small things such as these – not to mention boilers, coffee, farts, beer and bees.

To collect these sayings is – some would say – nothing new. This is both true and untrue. More than two hundred and fifty years ago, the French philosopher Voltaire (1694–1778) published his *Dictionnaire philosophique* (1764), which included entries on adultery, mountains, nakedness and many other unphilosophical matters. A book by another Frenchman of more recent vintage, *Mythologies* by Roland Barthes (1915–80), published in 1957, contained philosophical reflections on matters spanning from wrestling, through striptease, to the then new Citroën DS.

But these books encompassed mainly these two thinkers' own reflections and not those of other great minds. And, while we are at it, the American logician W. V. Quine published *Quiddities*, with the subtitle *An Intermittently Philosophical Dictionary*, which cited Voltaire's book as an inspiration. Quine's book is witty, occasionally weird and often wonderful. Yet, despite its title, this book deals with rather complex issues such as Gödel's Theorem, Fermat's ditto and spacetime, which are all fascinating but also rather high-brow. *Great Minds on Small Things* differs, therefore, from these earlier volumes in being a collection – perhaps the world's first – of the sayings, remarks and utterances on life's mundanities by some of the most famous philosophers of all time. Now, you may consider this an entirely frivolous endeavour and a rather pointless one at that. That is perhaps the case, and, in many ways, I am unapologetic. Why not just have fun and read things for the sake of it?

In addition to being literally 'useless', this book also offers up thoughts that call on the reader to reflect and to philosophise for her, him or themselves, since many of the entries are linked to more general debates and discussions. So, while not a reference book, or even a volume that is likely ever to be on reading lists in liberal arts colleges, it might be of interest to those who are bored with the standard texts but who still love the wonderfully mad minds that have shaped the world of ideas down the centuries.

Occasionally, there may be technical philosophical terms, like 'empiricist' or 'ontology', and so on. These are marked with an asterisk, and for these words there is a short – non-technical – explanation at the end of the book.

Some thinkers have been more prone than others to thinking the philosophically unthinkable – or the plainly odd: Aristotle, for instance, because he wrote reams and reams during his lifetime, and Wittgenstein because, well, he was Wittgenstein. Some of the remarks you may find profound and insightful, but others are obviously barmy and demonstrate that great minds were sometimes rather strange – and even, frankly, wrong.

Sharp-eyed readers will notice that the entries are mostly drawn from Western philosophers – and mostly dead white men at that. Sadly, many female writers of the past were not given their due and, indeed, were not published, or were published but have since fallen into near-complete obscurity. But this has been changing in recent years. For this reason, many of the women writers quoted in this book were working in the twentieth century. Most of the entries, likewise, are penned by those of the European tradition, with the exception of a few intriguing quotations from the likes of Confucius, Laozi and others. But in the main, the writers and thinkers quoted are from the tradition of the *Abendland* – the evening lands – as the Germans poetically call the West. This, once again, is *not* because thinkers of Eastern or other traditions were not profound or prolific. It merely reflects the undersigned's training and background. I hope that someone with deeper knowledge of these other global traditions will be able to complement this volume in the future.

The entries in this little volume are in alphabetical order – just like Voltaire's *Dictionnaire*. In collecting them, no particular method was followed.

Over the years – indeed, decades – while preparing and teaching classes in the history of the ideas or philosophy, I was often struck by the odd asides contained in some of the greatest and most famous books of the Western canon. I wrote these down in my notebooks, and many of these scribbles are now collected here. Some of the entries in this book are adapted from articles I have penned over the years for my regular column in the magazine *Philosophy Now*, but most of them I have not written about before. So, welcome to the weird and – I think – wonderful world of the greatest minds on life's smallest matters. This dictionary may not help you much if you are pursuing a career as an academic philosopher, but it is to be hoped that you will be surprised – perhaps occasionally shocked – but entertained throughout by these irreverent musings on mundanity.

Matthew Qvortrup
Kew
October 2023

ALE – see BEER

ANIMALS

It is said that Friedrich Nietzsche (1844–1900), on the brink of madness, once embraced a horse. It had been cruelly whipped by its master. The German philosopher felt it was his duty to apologise for its plight, indirectly caused by his fellow thinkers and above all, his long-dead colleague René Descartes (1596–1650), he of 'I think-therefore-I-am' fame – in case you have forgotten.

The Frenchman, as you may or may not know, had suggested that animals were like sophisticated mechanical clocks and were therefore devoid of reason. Basically, Descartes contended, they were machines, and could for this reason be treated like inanimate objects. In a letter to an English gentleman, the French philosopher set out his ideas:

> I know that animals do many things better than we do, but this does not surprise me. It can even be used to prove they act naturally and mechanically, like a clock which tells the time better than our judgement does. Doubtless when the swallows come in spring, they operate like clocks.[1]

There are horror stories about the Frenchman dissecting his wife's dog while it was still alive. This is a vicious, unsubstantiated rumour. For starters, Descartes never married, and he treated his pet dog, Monsieur Grat (Mr Scratch) – as the canine was called – with affection. So, he was anything but cruel in practical life. But it's true that, at a more philosophical level, he did not think much of the inner lives of our four-legged friends – or other animals for that matter.

> Though there are many animals which manifest more industry than we in certain of their

> actions, [this] does not prove that they are endowed with mind, for it would thence follow that they possessed greater reason than any of us ... On the contrary, it rather proves that they are destitute of reason, and that it is nature which acts in them according to the disposition of their organs: thus it is seen, that a clock composed only of wheels and weights can number the hours and measure time more exactly than we with all our skin.[2]

Though Descartes was rather more subdued in life than his cruel reputation suggests, his view represented a setback for animals and their rights. Immediately after the rationalist* French philosopher had made his pronouncements, Bishop George Berkeley (1685–1753), an Irish philosopher of the empiricist* persuasion, made a similar observation: 'we have no Grounds to think Brutes have Abstract general Ideas,' he wrote.[3] For people like Berkeley, 'ideas' meant thoughts. So, essentially, he took the same approach as Descartes. Yet the Irish bishop generally fared better reputationally, and he was not singled out for his meanness towards animals. It was for Descartes's sins – not for those of Berkeley – that Nietzsche sought to atone.

Nietzsche had reason for apologising, at least if we focus on the philosophy of the seventeenth and early eighteenth centuries. Things were going downhill for our animal friends at this time. Descartes and Berkeley's descriptions of animals as inanimate objects marked a turning point. Was this attitude towards animals cultural, perhaps, or was it a sign of the times?

It is widely, if erroneously, assumed that we were more primitive in the medieval period, which began with the fall of Rome in 476 CE. We tend to believe that these were the dark ages when our ancestors were burning witches and lived in constant terror of the torment in a physically existing hell after death. In fact, many of these ideas were *more* widespread *after* 1500 CE, when the 'modern' period conventionally began.

On the topic of animals, the Middle Ages were more progressive and enlightened than the supposedly 'rational' minds of the early modern period. For example, the Persian philosopher commonly known in the West as Avicenna – real name Ibn Sina

(980–1037) – was much more positive as regards the intelligence of beasts, believing that they were aware of themselves through their material organs.[4] So, perhaps, Western philosophers were simply more intolerant and less likely to be members of the RSPCA – or whatever the equivalent was in those days. Do Descartes and Berkeley perhaps exemplify familiar Western rationality run amok? Certainly, if we look even further east, the view of animals was frankly much kinder and more enlightened, and had been so for a long time. The Chinese sage Laozi (604–517 BCE), was, it seems, a gentle soul who liked animals as much as people. 'Be good to people … and to animals! Do not incite people or animals, nor harm them,' runs one of the aphorisms attributed to him. So, is the materialistic philosophy of the West to blame? Not really. In fact, Descartes and Berkeley proved to be exceptions to the general rule. And things had well and truly moved on by Nietzsche's time.

As a classical scholar, Nietzsche would have known that many of the ancient thinkers were much more open-minded in their view of animals. Going back all the way to the Greeks, Plato was in no doubt that animals had minds of their own. For otherwise their behaviour did not make sense. As Socrates – Plato's avatar in his great works of philosophical dialogue – asks in his familiar rhetorical style, 'Will any animal, a horse, a dog, or any other be ready to be brave, if it is not strong in spirit?[5] Clearly not, he thought.

Aristotle (384–322 BCE) too took that view that animals had souls, though some were more intelligent than others, 'in a general way in the lives of animals

many resemblances to human life may be observed. Acute intelligence will be seen more in smaller creatures than in large ones, as is exemplified of birds by the nest-building of the swallow'.[6]

This view was not merely an ancient one. Shortly after Descartes and Berkeley's writings, things began to look up for our fellow creatures, and philosophers began to go back to the views espoused by the Greek masters.

David Hume (1711–76), for example, took a view that was directly opposite to that of Descartes. He wrote that 'no truth appears to me more evident than that beasts are endow'd with thought and reason'. And, perhaps as a dig at Descartes, the Scottish philosopher went on to say that 'the arguments are in this case so obvious that they never escaped the most stupid and ignorant'.[7]

Immanuel Kant (1724–1804) was generally in disagreement with his Scottish colleague on pretty much everything. But the two agreed on animals. The philosopher from Königsberg even went so far as to suggest that 'The violent and cruel treatment of animals is contrary to man's duty to himself, because it dulls compassion and weakens and gradually eradicates a disposition very conducive to morality'.[8]

But there were always sceptics. By the late 1940s, Ludwig Wittgenstein (1889–1951) was still uncertain when he wrote, 'the dog means something by wagging its tail. What grounds could one give for saying this? We would hardly ask if the crocodile means something when it comes at a man with open jaws'.[9] Maybe the Austrian believed that animals could be inanimate objects. Maybe there was still a need to hug more horses and apologise for misdeeds against animals. In the twenty-first century most philosophers have learned their lesson and take care to show concern for animals. No one more so than the Australian philosopher Peter Singer (b. 1946), who even wrote a book on the topic entitled *Animal Liberation: A New Ethics for the Treatment of Animals* (1975), in which he argued that animals should be treated with respect because they are capable of suffering. Singer said that it was his experiences as a young man studying in England that turned him into an animal rights activist. All of which reminds me of my friend who lost his job as a fundraiser for an animal rights charity which shall here remain nameless. Why did he lose his job? Well, he said getting people to donate was like flogging a dead horse.

ARTICHOKE

Ludwig Wittgenstein was one of the rare philosophers to remark on the humble artichoke, and – of course – he made a philosophical point in the process: 'In order to find the real artichoke, we divested it of its leaves … [But] what is essential … is not [what is] hidden within'.[10] Well, excuse me for saying so, but it seems that the philosopher was not much of a cook. Surely, it is within the artichoke that we find what is edible.

B

BASEBALL

Many philosophers were remarkably – and perhaps surprisingly – athletic (see: SPORT). John Rawls (1921–2002) played college football – of the American variety – for Princeton. But he is more commonly regarded as the foremost of American political philosophers, and even as the man who single-handedly resurrected the whole discipline of political philosophy, which had fallen into oblivion after philosophers in Britain, Australia and North America became analytic* and obsessed with the meaning of words.

Rawls's first love, however, was not football but that other great American sport, baseball. So, what did Rawls do and what on God's earth have his writings got to do with the sport of Joe DiMaggio – aka 'Jolting Joe' – and Babe Ruth?

Well, first things first. In his book *A Theory of Justice* (1971), Rawls introduced the idea that our ethical* ideas (theories of good and bad) have to be weighed against our gut feelings to find what he called 'a reflective equilibrium'.[11]

And this is where baseball comes in. In fact, the whole idea grew out of the philosopher's reflections on America's favourite pastime, for he adopted the same argument about reflective equilibrium for his philosophy of baseball. In his article 'Two Concepts of Rules', published in *Philosophical Review* in 1955, he used examples of 'the ballgame' to explain his general philosophy, and in a separate letter to a friend he elaborated on why baseball was, in his mind, the best of all games. He wrote:

> The rules of the game are in equilibrium: that is, from the start, the diamond was made just the right size, the pitcher's mound just the right distance from home plate, etc., and this makes possible the marvellous plays, such as the double play. The physical layout of the game is perfectly adjusted to the human skills

> it is meant to display and to call into graceful exercise. Whereas, basketball, e.g., is constantly – or was then – adjusting its rules to get them in balance.

Rawls wanted everyone to have a decent chance in life, and he was pretty big on fairness. He suggested that a fair society would be the one we would come up with if we didn't know if we were each rich or poor, black or white, male or female. Again, baseball fitted the bill as an analogy because 'the game does not give unusual preference or advantage to special physical types, e.g., to tall men as in basketball. All sorts of abilities can find a place somewhere, the tall and the short etc. can enjoy the game together in different positions'.[12] For complementary reasons, Rawls did not like basketball, because it unfairly favoured tall men – like Rawls himself, as it happens: he was over 6'2".

Perhaps Rawls had another, unspoken motivation to single out this sport, since his rival, the libertarian philosopher Robert Nozick (1938–2002), used the example of the famous basketball player Wilt Chamberlain to justify income inequality.[13]

Nozick did not mind that some enjoyed greater advantages due to accidents of birth, such as their height. Rawls wanted equality. Nozick did not. So, in a sense, modern political philosophy – and perhaps the differences between conservatives and liberal progressives – can be reduced to whether you are a fan of basketball or baseball.

BATH

'I have a bath in the evening,' announced the French existentialist Simone de Beauvoir (1908–86) in an interview with the *Observer* newspaper in March 1960. 'I find it relaxing.' Why the left-leaning paper wanted to know about her bathing habits and not something more substantial is anyone's guess.[14] They could have enquired which of her best ideas had come to Beauvoir while she was performing her ablutions. Sadly, that was not what they asked. But before we get to the meaty philosophical questions, let's start with a few statistics. Today, we know that sixty-two per cent of Brits wash at least once each day, and that they spend on average 7–8 minutes under the shower.[15] Surveys also tell us that eighty-three per cent of those who take a bath in the morning reported being 'productive each day', while only seventy-eight per cent of those who had a bath in the evening did. There's a long history of bright ideas emerging from behind the bathroom door. A recent study sponsored by a German manufacturer, meanwhile, found that seventy-two per cent of respondents claimed to have creative ideas while in the shower.[16] So, based on this evidence, we could infer that Simone Lucie Ernestine Marie Bertrand de Beauvoir – to give the French philosopher her full and rather impressive name – could have been more productive if she had changed her habits.

Whether or not you believe in such statistical jiggery-pokery, most of us know instinctively that baths often stimulate deep thoughts. Arthur Schopenhauer (1788–1860) was German, of course, and had many ideas – not all of them good, mind you. Schopenhauer was known as a pessimist. He believed that the world was driven forward by a force that he called 'the Will', and which he defined as 'the deepest essence, the core, of every single thing', which 'appears in every blinding force of nature'.[17] For him, the world was irrational and pointless, and we could only partially escape from our sorry predicament through the enjoyment of art and music. Inspired by Indian religion, and especially by his reading of the *Bhagavad Gita*, the most revered of the Hindu texts, he concluded that the world entirely consisted of this 'Will', and that even the representation of external reality was tricked by it. (Modern readers who enjoy movies will recall that these sorts of ideas are explored in Lilly and Lana Wachowski's philosophical science-fiction film *The Matrix*.) So far, so good. But how did Schopenhauer come up with this idea? Well, it came to him in the bath. He said as much. In order to think clearly, he wrote, 'what is required is … a cold bath', as this helps with 'calming down … the blood circulation and the passionate nature'.[17]

Schopenhauer hated his compatriot Georg Wilhelm Friedrich Hegel (1770–1831). The latter was more successful, and as it happens a nicer human being, who helped his friends if they ended up in jail. But as much as Schopenhauer and Hegel were on opposite sides in philosophical debates, they agreed on the benefits of having a bath. Certainly, being clean can lead to serene tranquillity, as Hegel believed, and for this reason he admired the Egyptians, for 'they wash and bathe much, and undergo cleansing every month', which, he added, 'points to a condition of settled peace'.[18]

Not only the ancient Egyptians but also the Romans, as we well know, enjoyed getting their kit off and having a bath. This predilection was yet another of the things they picked up from the Greeks. But not everyone in the classical world enjoyed the experience. The Stoic philosopher Epictetus (55–135) was not particularly enthusiastic about going to the baths. He worried about 'the splashing of water, the crowding, the scolding, the stealing'. He was tempted not to go but, in line with his philosophy, adopted a, well, stoic approach, and counselled his reader:

> You will more steadily engage in the activity if you honestly say 'I want to bathe and want to hold my will in accordance with nature'. And so it should be for every action. So if anything happens when I am in the bath, I will cheerfully say 'I did not only want this, but I also wanted to hold my will in accordance with nature; and I will not hold it like that if I am annoyed about what happens'.[19]

We can infer that he took the plunge.

Hannah Arendt (1906–75) did not share his fears of chaos at the bathhouse – for her and her friends, the bathtub was clearly a place to relax and read. In a letter she thanked Sonia Orwell – George Orwell's wife, who inspired him to write *1984* – for sending her bathing oil, while Arendt's close friend Mary McCarthy – the celebrated author of *The Group* – wrote to the philosopher that she had read her book *On the Origins of Totalitarianism* in the bath.[20]

BEER

The Germans – this will not be a surprise – are rather fond of their lager. Too much so, thought Friedrich Nietzsche. 'How much lager is in the German intelligentsia!' he lamented, and continued by pondering, 'How is it possible that young men who dedicate their existence to the most spiritual goals do not feel the first instinct of spirituality, the instinct of self-preservation of the spirit – and drink beer?'[21]

It's possible that Nietzsche had Martin Luther (1483–1546) in mind. The bookish theologian certainly dedicated his life to 'spiritual goals', and reportedly observed, 'Those who do not drink beer, have nothing to drink'.

But beer drinking is not confined to just one nation. We, too, like a drink on these islands – though not in equal amounts. One NHS study found that the Scottish drink more beer than the English.[22] But their data stand at odds with the anecdotal evidence of our canonical philosophers because David Hume (born in Edinburgh) had an aversion to ale, while his English colleague John Locke loved the stuff to the extent that he even authored a book on the subject.

David Hume observed that you could write poetry about cider. But, the Scottish thinker went on, 'Beer would not have been so proper as being neither agreeable to the taste nor eye.'[7] John Locke, who was English, took a rather different view. In 1679 he penned his *Classification of Beer.* In this meticulous – and of course strictly empirical – study, Locke divided beer into three categories: home-made, for sale and compound.

He found – undoubtedly following experimentation – that 'Home-made drinks of England are beer and ale, strong and small; those of most note, that are to be sold, are Lambeth ale, Margaret ale, and Derby ale; Herefordshire cider, perry, mede. There are also several sorts of compounded ales, as cock-ale, wormwood-ale, lemon-ale, scurvygrass-ale, college-ale, &c. These are to be had at Hercules Pillars, near the Temple; at the Trumpet, and other houses in Sheer Lane, Bell Alley, and, as I remember, at the English Tavern, near Charing Cross'.[23]

Is it just me, or do you also fancy a pint?

BEES

The title of *The Fable of the Bees* by the Dutch physician Bernard Mandeville (1670–1733) might suggest some sort of zoologically minded study of social relations among our stripy, nectar-gathering insect friends. But in fact, with the subtitle *Private Vices, Publick Benefits*, this 1714 book is a witty allegory about the supposed virtues of selfishness, which in turn inspired the likes of Adam Smith (1723–90), Friedrich Hayek (1899–1992) and Margaret Thatcher (1925–2013).

However, other thinkers have been fascinated, even enamoured, by actual bees. Francis Bacon (1561–1626) wrote that 'the bee, a mean between both [ant

and spider], extracts matter from the flowers of the garden and the field, but works and fashions it by its own effort. The true labor of philosophy resembles hers...'[24] Bacon is generally seen as the first modern philosopher to write in a scientific way and to break with the tradition of Aristotle. His book was called the 'new' *Organon* to distinguish it from Aristotle's much earlier book, which was called simply *Organon* – a Greek word that means 'tool' or 'instrument'.

Yet, the English philosopher and scientist was not so different from the old master. Indeed, their descriptions were rather similar, and Aristotle, as was his wont, was very detailed. 'Of bees', he said, 'there are various species', and he went on:

> The best kind is a little round mottled insect; another is long and resembles the anthrena; a third is a black and flat-bellied, and is nick-named the 'robber'; a fourth kind is the drone, which is the largest of all bees, but it is inactive and it doesn't sting. And this proportionate size of the drone explains why some bee-masters place a mesh barrier in front of the hives to

> keep the big drones out while it lets the little bees go in.[6]

Thomas Hobbes (1588–1679), also namechecked the small and sociable animal in his greatest work and wrote that

> Certain living creatures, as Bees … live sociably one with another, (which are therefore by Aristotle numbred amongst Politicall creatures;) and yet have no other direction, than their particular judgements and appetites; nor speech, whereby one of them can signifie to another, what he thinks expedient for the common benefit.[25]

Even Søren Kierkegaard (1813–55) pondered the work of bees – albeit merely to reflect on the nature of a great work of art. In his early masterpiece *Either/Or*, he argued that art is the work of a genius, and what is beautiful is consciously made, for if this were not to be the case, then honeycomb would be the work of geniuses.[26] But, perhaps, Kierkegaard's premise was wrong. Why exactly must a great work of art be the outcome of a single individual? Isn't it exactly the very ability to act socially and create something through common endeavour that is, well, the genius of bees? And more generally, can art be created by the many?

Modern research suggests that something akin to referendums are known in the animal kingdom – though without the polarisation that often characterises voting on single issues among humans. 'When a honeybee swarm chooses its future home, it practices the form of democracy known as direct democracy, in which the individuals within a community who choose to participate in its decision making do so personally rather than through representatives,' writes Thomas D. Seeley in his book *Honeybee Democracy*.[27] Bees certainly are what Aristotle termed a *zoon politikon* – a political animal. And that is why many of us – philosophers included – find them so inspirational.

BIRTHMARKS

Descartes had an elaborate, even outlandish theory: 'Birthmarks,' he noted, 'never occur in the infant when the mother eats fruits which she likes,' and for this reason, the Frenchman speculated, 'it is quite probable that they can sometimes be cured when the infant eats the fruit in question.'[28] This was his theory. Descartes was not really a man who tested things in practice. He preferred to sit in front of the fireplace and cogitate. Maybe he was right. I personally doubt it. But who knows? Don't dismiss a theory out of hand because it seems odd!

BOILERS

We all want to keep warm in the winter. Even the most otherworldly of philosophers. As we saw in the preceding entry, Descartes hated the cold and wrote his *Meditations* in front of the fire. Perhaps he thought, 'I feel warm, therefore I am.' Central heating systems didn't exist in Descartes's time – we can imagine much to his disappointment – but three hundred years later, Wittgenstein devoted a surprising amount of space in arguably his most influential book to the subject of, yes, boilers.

The famously austere Wittgenstein's rooms at Cambridge University were always cold. Perhaps that is why, when considering why we think, his thoughts turned to boilers. Oddly, there was no central heating at the university in the early 1950s, even though the boiler system had been patented in the US in 1867, and central heating was known in Wittgenstein's native Vienna. He had originally trained in mathematics and mechanical engineering and was deeply unimpressed by his British colleagues' lack of aptitude for mental arithmetic and algebra. Perhaps this explained, in his mind, why these devices were so rare in England at the time, for he wrote: 'boilers do not explode so often if made according to precise calculations. So, ultimately, we resort to calculations because it makes practical sense.' For 'having once been burnt [we] would do anything rather than put [our] hands into a fire'.[9] Whether it was due to poor mathematical skills or exploding boilers, central heating did not become commonplace in England until the 1970s, some twenty years after Wittgenstein's death. But we are left to wonder whether, if it had been available at Cambridge back then, that notoriously parsimonious and otherworldly philosopher would even have bothered to turn the radiators on.

BREAD

These days, the terms Epicureanism and hedonism – the broader strand of philosophy of which Epicureanism was a subset – tend to be understood as denoting extreme sensory gratification of one kind or another and are generally associated with sexual pleasure and living to excess. This school of philosophy was established by the Greek philosopher Epicurus (341–270 BCE).

But, in fact, though Epicurus and his followers understood pleasure as life's chief good and goal, theirs was a strictly controlled vision. 'Barley bread and water yield the peak of pleasure,' he wrote.[29] He advised that 'plain fare gives as much pleasure as a costly diet'.[30] Forget *la dolce vita*, and read what the man said himself. Stick to simple bread. Other philosophers have written about bread too. 'Acorns were good before bread was found,' runs a quote often attributed to Francis Bacon, who also liked this foodstuff. Mary Wollstonecraft (1759–97) was less concerned about the product itself and more focused on the fact that women 'pass their whole lives working for their daily bread'.[31] And Buddha – in his Zen incarnation – reputedly said that 'the bread in our hand is the body of the cosmos'. The Prophet Muhammad is cited – perhaps apocryphally – as saying 'bread feeds the body but flowers feed the soul', while the Christian Bible has a lot to say about the stuff, from our 'daily bread' in the Lord's Prayer (Matthew 6:11) to Jesus's miraculous loaves, as recorded in the Gospels. Wherever they're coming from, no one seems to have had a bad word to say about bread. And unlike the product itself, these quotes will never turn stale.

BREAKFAST

'I was thinking about my breakfast and wondering whether it would be late today...'[9] Wittgenstein, ready to tuck into his eggs and pastries, would have found himself at odds with his thirteenth-century colleague Thomas Aquinas (1225–74). The friar, who was otherwise rather relaxed about excessive food consumption, regarded it a sin to eat breakfast too early and even invented the term *praepropere*, meaning to eat too soon, or at an improper time.[32]

Hume, on the other hand, was in the Wittgenstein camp. He liked to break his fast early and well, and considered it a 'good symptom' to 'have a very ravenous appetite'.[33] To fuel another day of philosophical musings, he would happily have joined Wittgenstein in falling upon the *Frühstück*. So, as the Austrian would say, *Guten Appetit*!

BUILDINGS

The English have always been a very practical lot. Francis Bacon was a case in point: 'Houses are built to live in and not to look on,' he wrote in an essay devoted to the subject.[24] The same pragmatic sentiment was evident when Mary Wollstonecraft wrote about buildings in *A Vindication of the Rights of Women*. The ur-feminist would not have had a lot of time for the ubiquitous DIY programmes that fill up our television screens: 'whatever appearance the house and garden may make on children they do not enjoy either'.[31] David Hume, likewise, stressed the practical over the aesthetic. Sounding rather as if he was recounting an episode of *Grand Designs* or *Location, Location, Location*, Hume described how 'A man who shows us any house or building, takes particular care, among other things, to point out the convenience of the apartments, the advantages of their situation, and the little room lost in the stairs, anti-chambers and passages'.[7]

That the continental philosophers, from Descartes to Heidegger and Wittgenstein, held a different view is almost to be expected. Hegel took the antithetical view that 'architecture is fine art' – and even went on in a highly metaphysical tone to note that a 'building is the first to open the way for the adequate actuality of the god'.[34]

René Descartes was a bit more down to earth when he wrote about houses, though he too had strong views. 'Buildings undertaken and completed by a single architect,' wrote the French rationalist, 'are usually more beautiful and better ordered than those that have several draftsmen'.[2]

The cabin designed and built by Martin Heidegger (1889–1976) was in its own way 'beautiful'. *Die Hütte* ('The Hut') in the Black Forest is now open to the public. It is an aesthetically pleasing three-bedroom sanctuary for thinking – though without the comforts that were standard even in the 1920s. Heidegger the master-builder reflected that his thinking about building did not presume to discover any architectural ideas, let alone to provide rules for how to build.[35]

Heidegger was not the only philosopher to dabble in a bit of building. He had few similarities with Wittgenstein philosophically. The former was a quintessential continental* thinker, while the latter was the foremost of the analytical philosophers. But the two men, who were born in the same year, shared one passion: building and architecture. Heidegger got his hands dirty and was a practitioner. Wittgenstein, by contrast, was content with directing his workers and never took part in the construction labour itself. He seems rather detached when he writes about the art of building houses. 'Architecture,' he opined, 'immortalizes and glorifies [and] there can be no architecture where there is nothing to glorify.'[36] Glorious or not, the philosopher designed a house for his sister, and had it built – he came from a very well-to-do family. The house still stands in Kundmanngasse in Vienna. His sister, however, hated the building and never lived there. Interestingly, Wittgenstein, who was never entirely comfortable with the epithet 'philosopher', was listed in the Vienna City Telephone Directory as Dr L. Wittgenstein, architect.

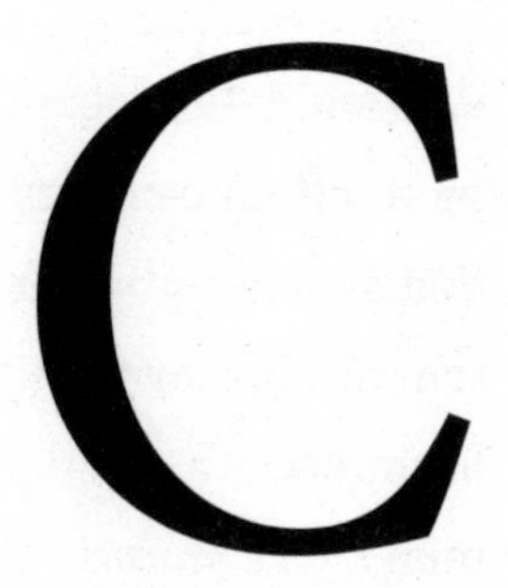

CARS

For obvious reasons, Plato, Kant and Hume did not write about motorcars. But we know what Bertrand Russell thought about cars because he – being a twentieth-century philosopher – published his reflections on them. In an essay dating back to 1927, he mused on cars as a means of understanding our often irrational behaviour towards our fellow human beings.

> No man treats a motorcar as foolishly as he treats another human being. When the car will not go, he does not attribute its annoying behaviour to sin; he does not say, 'You are a wicked motorcar, and I shall not give you any more petrol until you go.' He attempts to find out what is wrong and to set it right.[37]

Perhaps it did not appear to Lord Russell that the car is an inanimate object? Hannah Arendt was in no doubt that a car is but a thing, and while we have no evidence that the author of *Eichmann in Jerusalem* was a petrol-head, she was alert in one of her most philosophical books, *The Human Condition*, to our voracious enthusiasm for our new invention, consumed 'as though [cars] were the "good things" of nature'.[38]

CATS

'I am the animal that my cat sees,' the French philosopher Jacques Derrida (1930–2004) reportedly said.[39] French philosophers disagreed on everything: communism, structuralism, being, nothingness, revolution, and the list goes on. But on one thing they agreed. An important one. They were all cat people. And they gave their mousers rather appropriate names. Take but three examples. Jean-Paul Sartre (1905–80) had a cat named Néant. Which, of course, was one of the titular terms in his dense treatise *Being and Nothingness* from 1943. Not to be outdone, Michel Foucault (1926–84) named his black cat Insanity – needless to say, he rather had to call her that, as he was the author of *Madness and Civilisation* (1961). Jacques Derrida is often pictured with Logos. Maybe his famous critique of 'logocentrism' was really a way of telling himself that his grey feline ruled his life?[40]

Other philosophical traditions were less feline-friendly. Not least the Germans. 'A black tom-cat, with its glowing eyes and its now gliding, now quick and darting movement, has been deemed the presence of a malignant being – a mysterious reserved spectre,' wrote Hegel.[18] It can probably be fairly concluded that the German philosopher was not a 'cat person'. Though he rather liked canines (see: DOG).

The German physicist Erwin Schrödinger (1887–1961) is perhaps most famous nowadays for his (theoretical) cat, whose state of mortality is impossible to determine with certainty from outside its sealed box. But this thought experiment, devised with Albert Einstein to explore the problem of quantum superposition, is more alarming than most people commonly remember: not only was the learned professor not a cat-owner himself, but the experiment he proposed in 'The Contemporary State of Quantum Mechanics' required the cat to be locked inside a steel chamber with a flask of poison and a source of radioactive atoms.[41] This, frankly, does not sound like the work of a cat lover, but rather a cause for concern and a swift phone call to the Cats Protection League. Nope, Schrödinger cannot have been feline-friendly.

Michel de Montaigne (1533–92) was, by contrast, a confirmed cat lover. In his famous *Essais*, he posed a question that is both a philosophical conundrum and an observation that will be instantly recognisable to any owner of an unfussed feline: 'When I play with my cat, it is an open question if she is not entertaining herself more playing with me than I am with her?'[42]

CHAIRS

Philosophers can be divided into so-called 'idealists'* and 'realists'.* For the former it is all in our heads – and it may not be happening in the 'real world'. For the latter the world out there exists independently of us. Wittgenstein, despite not having any children, could not help wondering whether it makes a difference if – like the idealist – a child thinks the chair is a mental phenomenon, or whether they believe – as realists do – that chairs exist independently of our perception of them. Wittgenstein went on, 'the Idealist will teach his children the word "chair". He wants to teach them to fetch the chair. But the question then arises, is there a difference between the idealist-educated children and the realist ones?'[9] Basically, is a chair a chair? Does it matter if you think that the chair is 'real', or if the chair – as the idealist would believe – is only a representation before your inner eye? Yes, this is a rather philosophical question. And maybe it just proves to you that philosophy is pointless. Or, perhaps, like me, you can spend hours thinking about it? Take your pick.

CHEESE

Grated cheese has been around longer than you might think. Plato, in *The Republic*, recounted a case of an injured man who was 'sprinkled with a large amount of barley and grated cheese', though he admitted that this 'was certainly an absurd concoction to give a man in that condition'.[5] It took nearly 2,000 years before a great mind wrote about cheeses again.

Gottfried Wilhelm Leibniz (1646–1716) was a universal genius – and was recognised as such. Indeed, no less a genius than Albert Einstein (1879–1955) called himself a 'Leibnizian'. The philosopher's most important contribution to metaphysics was the idea of monads. His theory of the indivisible non-materialist ultimate atom that is the basis of all things was rather complex and, in many ways, akin to the concepts of quantum physics. So, how did he explain it? Well, naturally, by invoking cheese. As he wrote to a sceptical colleague, 'I don't say that bodies which are commonly called inanimate, have perceptions and appetition, rather they have something of that sort in them, as worms in cheese'.[43] It's hard to say whether this really clarifies his position.

Our modest friend Epicurus (see: BREAD) evidently placed cheese high up the list of sanctioned pleasures: 'Send me a small pot of cheese, so that I may be able to indulge myself whenever I wish'.[44] Apparently, the Greek relied on his simple diet of goat's cheese. Our Epicurean appetites have come a long way since their namesake's time.

Goat's cheese, Jarlsberg, Camembert, you name it. It's all a matter of taste. John Locke pointed out that 'The mind has a different relish, as well as the palate, and you will as fruitlessly endeavour to … satisfy all men's hunger with cheese, which though very agreeable to some [is] to others extremely nauseous and offensive'.[45] Robert Louis Stevenson (1850–94), the author of *Treasure Island,* confided in his readers that 'many a long night, I've dreamed of cheese'.[46] Wittgenstein was a cheese fan too: the economist John Maynard Keynes (1883–1946) recalled that when the Austrian philosopher paid him a visit in 1929, he gave him 'Swiss cheese and rye bread for lunch, which he greatly liked. Thereafter he more or less insisted on eating bread and cheese at all meals.'[47]

It's said, however, that too much cheese gives you nightmares, and Plato certainly expressed concerns about its effects: 'You might condemn cheese out of hand when you have heard someone praise its merits as a food, without stopping to ask about its effects.'[48] Mary Wollstonecraft, meanwhile, wrote that those who have lived at sea on a diet of 'Cheese [were] feeling uncommon pains',[49] and reported from her travels in Sweden 'that *cheese* … was the bane of this country'.[50] But these warnings were not heeded by everyone. Kant loved the stuff so much that he reportedly *died* of a surfeit of cheese sandwiches.[51]

Yes, cheese is a weighty subject. After all, as the late French President Charles de Gaulle (1890–1970) put it, how can 'you govern a nation that has two-hundred and fifty-eight sorts of cheese?'[52] Good question, and one that citizens should bear in mind in a country like the UK, which has over 700 *variétés de fromage.* If the Frenchman was right, we should brace ourselves for imminent anarchy.

CHILDREN

'Children are the only brave philosophers. And brave philosophers are, inevitably, children,' the Russian science-fiction writer and philosopher Yevgeny Zamyatin (1884–1937) is often quoted as saying. Erasmus of Rotterdam (*c.*1466–1536) wrote a book on the education of children – though he had none – while two centuries later, Jean-Jacques Rousseau (1712–78), who also gained a reputation as an educationalist, gave all his own children away to a foundling home.

Like his compatriot Erasmus, the Dutch philosopher Benedict Spinoza (1632–77) was a bachelor and did not have much experience with children, but he seemed to have a straightforward understanding of them as being governed by their bodily impulses and 'equilibrium', claiming that 'children laugh or cry simply because they see others laughing or crying'.[53] Søren Kierkegaard, another bachelor-philosopher, took a more sardonic line on the virtues of children over grown-ups. 'I prefer to be in the company of children, for you can at least entertain the hope that they may one day grow up to become reasonable. As for those who have already become adults – Jesus Christ...'[26]

Descartes did not write about children. We can speculate that this was because it was too painful for him. The Frenchman, though he never married, fathered a daughter with his Dutch maid, Helena Jans van der Strom. But when little Francine died of scarlet fever at the age of five, Descartes was devastated, according to research recently published in the official *Bulletin Cartésien*.[54] Indeed, the death of Francine Descartes in 1640 spurred René to create an effigy in her likeness. For the author of *Principles of Philosophy* (1644), this lifeless object represented the grief and sadness that a parent suffers after the death of a child. Descartes was, it seems, a rather nice chap. When it became apparent that Helena could not marry him, he paid her dowry when she married a local artisan.[55]

Descartes was, as it happens, not the only philosopher to father a child out of wedlock. Hegel's landlady Christiana Fischer fell pregnant around the time when the then-penniless young philosopher published *The Phenomenology of the Spirit* (1807). Hegel, who wrote much about the 'ethical life', duly practised what he preached and paid alimony to support his son, Ludwig. Hegel, as a true dialectician, seems to have struck the right balance between tolerance and strictness as a parent. Mary Wollstonecraft was not a German idealist, but she would have agreed with him that a good parent neither 'neglect[s] children, or spoils them by improper indulgence'.[31]

CLOTHES

Some philosophers have been fashionistas. Aristotle, so Diogenes Laërtius (180–240) recorded, was a bit of a dandy, 'conspicuous by his attire, his rings, and the cut of his hair'.[56]

Simone de Beauvoir, by contrast, claimed that 'I am not at all interested in clothes'. Though paradoxically this remark was made during an interview for an article on 'My Clothes and I'. Her disinterest in garments might explain why she admitted that she 'never [got] dressed until midday' and did most of her writing in her dressing gown because – appropriately for an existentialist – 'one feels much freer'.[14]

Bertrand Russell was always dapper in his three-piece suit, and expressed bafflement that others could

take a different sartorial attitude. He found that one of 'the most curious changes in the men's attire' was the 'entirely new custom that only women cared about clothing, especially compared with former times'. He noted that the diarist Pepys, in the time of Charles II in the 1660s, spent far more on his own clothes than on those of his wife.[57]

COFFEE

Coffee brings clarity, and perhaps that is why Immanuel Kant swore by the black stuff. The Prussian *Meister* had quite particular habits. He would get up every morning at five, teach, then leave for his daily walk at precisely half-past three in the afternoon, dine with the same friend, and go to bed at precisely ten o'clock every night.

As for what he got up to in his waking hours, 'There were two things in life for which Kant had an intolerable liking: coffee and tobacco,' (see: TOBACCO) the English writer Thomas De Quincey (1785–1859) recounted in his famous biography *The Last Days of Immanuel Kant*.[58]

Wittgenstein, too, was a big coffee drinker. He had probably experienced good coffee in the cafés of his native Vienna. As a philosopher he was preoccupied with words. The word 'coffee' was a particular favourite:

> Describe the aroma of coffee. Why can't it be done? Do we lack the words? And *for what* are words lacking? But how do we get the idea that such a description must after all be possible? Have you ever felt the lack of such a description? Have you tried to describe the aroma of coffee and not succeeded?[10]

Iris Murdoch (1919–99), the English philosopher and novelist, did not share her colleagues' obsession, however: 'Coffee, unless it is very good and made by somebody else, is pretty intolerable at any time'.[59] Coffee must have been a bit of a preoccupation for philosophers in England at the time, for her contemporary Elizabeth Anscombe (1919–2001) made the observation that 'pouring out coffee when I meant to pour out tea' was a sentence that could be restated as 'pouring out liquid from this pot'.[60] Well, quite, but why replace a precise sentence with a less precise one? Anscombe never answered this question.

When the twenty-nine-year-old Kierkegaard penned his chef-d'oeuvre *Either/Or* he was pondering a very important existential question: to drink or not to drink coffee; either/or. For, as he explained, '… when I drink coffee, my nausea comes from drinking coffee, and when I do not drink coffee, my nausea comes from not drinking coffee. And so, with us humans. The whole earthly Life is a kind of malaise, in some the reason is too much effort, in others too little.'[26] Why such ill effects from his coffee drinking? The peculiar way he took it may explain this particular suffering. Contemporaries from Copenhagen in the 1840s recounted how Kierkegaard, 'delightedly … seized hold of the bag containing the sugar and poured sugar into the coffee cup until it was piled up above the rim. Next came the incredibly strong, black coffee, which slowly dissolved the white pyramid.'[61] Many of Kierkegaard's works have a certain – often ill-disguised – autobiographical element. One such was *The Repetition*, which concerns a young philosopher who studies for a semester in Berlin, as

Kierkegaard did. The student's account of his visit to the city's cafés places the emphasis on the coffee, not the company:

> I went out to the coffee-house, where on the previous visit [to Berlin], I went every day to enjoy the drink which according to the words of the poet, if it is 'pure and warm and strong and not abused,' can be placed alongside of that with which the poet compares it, namely, 'friendship'. I insist at least upon a good cup of coffee.[62]

Maybe a shot of caffeine was exactly what Kierkegaard needed. He had been a rather idle student in Copenhagen. But during his sojourn in Berlin in 1841, he managed to draft not only *Either/Or* (over 800 pages), but also his doctoral dissertation – *On the Concept of Irony with Continual Reference to Socrates* – in less than a year.

The French Enlightenment philosopher and novelist François-Marie Arouet, better known by his nom de plume Monsieur de Voltaire, reportedly drank fifty-five cups of coffee a day. Which seems remarkable. And, according to his physician, rather dangerous. When the doctor warned the eighty-year-old philosopher that his brew was a 'slow poison', Voltaire responded with characteristic wit, 'Yes, a very slow poison, indeed. I have been taking it every day for more than eighty years'.[63]

So, coffee is not necessarily unhealthy; in addition to being an intellectual stimulant, it can even be a simple, life-affirming, everyday pleasure. In her novel *The Mandarins* (1954), one of Simone de Beauvoir's characters lets slip that she will have a cup of coffee in the bistro on the corner and be back in a few minutes.[64] Very much the lifestyle we associate with the existentialists on the Left Bank. Now, what will you have: a latte, an espresso or a flat white?

COLD FEET

Aristotle was a great observer of the world, who investigated almost everything empirically. And based, one must assume, on detailed and controlled experiments, the great man concluded that 'it is either difficult or impossible to have sexual intercourse when the feet are not warm'.[65] Aristotle wrote rather a lot about feet, as it happens, and not all of it was related to the pleasures of the flesh. He also noted that 'of all the animals, man has the largest foot in proportion to the size of his body'.[66] Aristotle had never been to Australia, so he cannot have known about kangaroos who have – I think – longer feet. A good example of how any empirical researcher is limited by the available data.

COOKING

You may not read philosophy books expecting to find recipes. But you'd be surprised. Socrates (470–399 BCE) – who rather looked as if he liked his food – came close to giving us a recipe: 'they will have salt, olives and cheese, also boil up roots and herbs, the sort of vegetables they boil up in the country, and … we shall add to these dried figs, chickpeas and beans; they will roast myrtle berries and acorns in the ashes near the fire.[5] What this dish was called, let alone what it tasted like, is not reported.

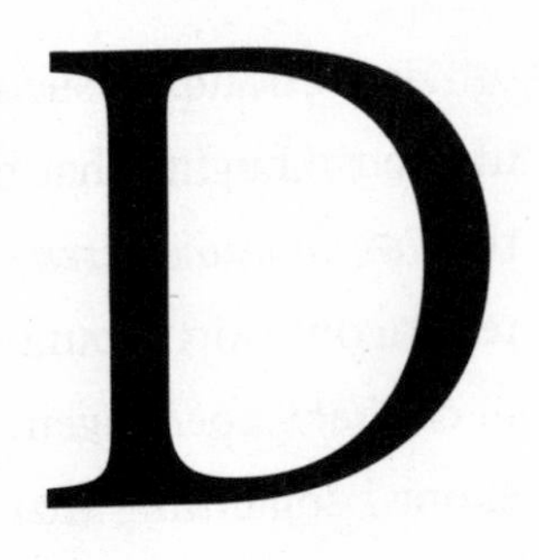

DANCE

Nietzsche – though the son of a Lutheran pastor – famously declared that 'God is Dead'. Yet he was not as doctrinaire as you might imagine. He was willing to reconsider his position regarding the existence of the Lord, if only the Almighty had moves. 'I would … believe in a God who knew how to dance,' he admitted. Why was he willing to ditch his principles and make this exception? Well, for starters because the otherwise bookish German was positively crazy about dancing. In his most famous book, he wrote – appropriately in a section entitled *Tanzlied* ('Dancing song') – 'Only in dance do I know how to speak parables of the highest things.' And, he went as far as to say, 'wasted is each day when you have not danced at least once.'[67]

Dance occupied such a prime place in Kierkegaard's life and thoughts that he was known by his compatriots as *dansemesteren* – the dance master. He would reportedly skip around Sortedam, the artificial lake in central Copenhagen. For Kierkegaard, dance could express something that other artforms could not. In *The Repetition*, a strange book that defies categorisation, he describes a man – who resembles the philosopher himself – who feels that:

> No wealth of language, no passion of exclamation was sufficient for him, when no expression, no gesticulation satisfied, when nothing contented him except to break out with the strangest leaps and somersaults. Perhaps the same individual learned to dance, perhaps he often saw ballets and admired the art of the dancer.[62]

In any case, Kierkegaard hoped 'always to be able to dance lightly in the service of thought'.[68] For the existentialist Dane, dance was a recurrent metaphor for life; he opined that 'most people live completely absorbed in the joys and sorrows of life, they are benchwarmers who do not take part in the dance'.[69]

Being an empiricist, Locke was more concerned with the educational aspects of dance than the existential or even spiritual ones. But he couldn't quite help making aesthetic judgements as well: 'Dancing being that which gives graceful motions to life,' he wrote, 'cannot be learned too early'. However, Locke was clear that one couldn't hope to be a good dancer without some tuition: 'You must make sure to have a good master, that knows and can teach what is graceful'. Getting down to the nitty-gritty, he specified that 'the jiggering part, and the figures of dances ... tends to perfect graceful carriage'.[70]

Whether Plato liked to cut some rug is not known. It seems unlikely. He was a bit of a bore. The Athenian admitted that there 'were movements of the body, which [are] described as "dancing in delight"', but he was far from interested in the joy of this activity. Dance should not be banned and was to be tolerated on the mechanistic grounds that it would 'result in a fine state of physical fitness'.[48] Al-Farabi – an admirer of Plato – took a more ageist view, stating that 'It is not suitable for an elderly person to ... dance'.[71]

Arendt, on the other hand, had more in common with Nietzsche and Kierkegaard – on the subject of dancing, at least. For her, dancing was associated with freedom, and she thought we must push through our inhibitions. As she explained, 'to stop in the midst of the consummation means not completing ... Anyone who wishes to dance the fandango and ceases in the midst of it from awkwardness or lack of strength, has not carried out an act of freedom'.[72]

So don't stop the dancing! Indeed, continue, for as the Russian-born anarchist and writer Emma Goldman (1869–1940) is famously – and perhaps apocryphally – reputed to have said, 'If I can't dance, I don't want to be in your revolution.'[73]

DIARY (How to keep a)

It must be said that sometimes philosophers overthink. Something as mundane as keeping a diary would, for us ordinary mortals, not be a matter for involved speculation and analysis. But – inevitably – Wittgenstein felt that keeping track of his appointments required a scientific approach. His ponderings resulted in the following, 'When I calculate when I am free according to my diary, the calculation is fSINdx'.[74] Later in the same work, Dr Wittgenstein was unsure why he happened not to have any diary commitments on Fridays. His equation, it seems, did not quite work. Perhaps the answer was more prosaic than philosophical – let alone mathematical – namely that his colleagues were already downing tools for the weekend?

DISAPPOINTMENT

'Before one can really get a sense of what life is one must have learnt to put up with being disappointed.' This was how Søren Kierkegaard saw the matter.[62] He was not a particularly happy person, it should be said, so maybe he took consolation from this by concluding that 'The hoping individualities always have a more pleasant disappointment'.[75]

Well, that is an interesting theory. Whether it is plausible or not is another matter. Another existentialist thinker rejected this view and found Kierkegaard's line of reasoning improbable – keeping it short and to the point, Simone de Beauvoir concluded that a disappointment always remained just that, a disappointment. When things do *not* turn out the way you'd hoped, you have cause to be miffed, thwarted and sad. Kierkegaard used the Danish word '*skuffelse*' in his essays.[62] Many years later, Johannes Møllehave (1937–2021) – a Danish theologian and novelist who wrote extensively about his more famous compatriot – authored a discourse on 'Disappointments that didn't come true' (*Skuffelser der ikke gik i Opfyldelse*, 1987). There is something rather uplifting in this approach to life.

DOGS

Diogenes the Cynic (404–323 BCE) was known as 'the dog' – the ancient Greek word *kynikós* actually means dog.

The philosopher lived in a *pithos*, that is, a large ceramic storage container – and not, as is often reported, in a barrel – positioned next to the marketplace. He never wrote a line, but he found our four-legged friends superior to vainglorious humans, and he proudly proclaimed of himself, 'I fawn on those who give me anything, I bark at those who refuse, and I set my teeth in rascals.'[76] The circumstances of his death are contested, but some maintain it was the result of an infected dog bite, and after he died, the Corinthians memorialised him with a pillar topped with a marble sculpture of a dog.

So, was he a dog? Certainly, if you follow the logic of Benedict Spinoza. The Dutchman went back to first principles, stating in *Ethics* that 'a dog [is] an animal that barks'.[53] Germaine de Staël (1766–1817) would have agreed with Diogenes's assessment of the relative merits of pooches versus their owners: 'The more I see of men, the more I like dogs,' she is said to have remarked.

Around that time, there was a lot of love for dogs among the philosophers. 'A Dog ... appear[s] friendly and sympathizing,'[18] noted Hegel, another 'dog person'.

Others were less enamoured by man's – and woman's – reputed best friend. Certainly, Thomas Hobbes was not a dog lover. A man who had been bitten by a canine, the English philosopher believed, was infected by a 'poison', which would sooner or later 'convert him into a Dog'.[25] This certainly an interesting theory. However, it is also – to my knowledge – one that has not been proven in anything like conventional medical textbooks, and it seems strangely like the plot of the horror movie *An American Werewolf in London*.

Nowadays, people often want dogs with a pedigree. We do not know if Aristotle had a dog, but he certainly had more time for mongrels than for pure breeds. 'Dogs that are born of a mixed breed between these two [sheepdogs and Molossians] are remarkable for courage and endurance of hard labour,' he believed.[6] Wittgenstein, on the other hand, perceived some deficiencies in the whole doggy setup. Pondering their inner lives, he asked 'Why a dog can feel fear and not remorse' … He believed he had found the answer. It was 'because they can't talk'.[9]

DRUNKENNESS

The relationship between Islam and drunkenness is – to put it diplomatically – uneasy.

But al-Farabi (870–950), the founder of Islamic philosophy, was not too doctrinaire: 'the situation that necessarily calls for drinking wine is that in which one needs to to be deprived of intellect or cognisance, for instance in childbirth … and painful doctoring of the body'.[71]

Michel de Montaigne – perhaps because he hailed from the refined wine-growing region of Bordeaux

– wrote a whole essay on drunkenness, which he considered 'among vices to be gross and coarse'. He claimed 'I do not much care for drinking but as following eating and washing down my meal'.[42] Going further back, Plato was not averse to a bit of booze, but he agreed that 'Drunkenness is most unbecoming', stressing that we should 'drink in moderation', and those who do it seems '...will spend their lives in peace and good health; they will reach old age and pass on to their successors a life just like this one'.[5]

Lucretius (99–55 BCE) was a metaphysical poet with a perceptive eye for the eternal truths. In rather unpoetic – but accurate – language he described how, 'when the wine has sunk in, our limbs become heavy, we stagger, we trip over our legs, our speech becomes slurred ... then comes the din, the hiccups, and the fights'.[77] Yes, the Saturday night scenes in ancient Rome were not so different from those on provincial high streets in twenty-first-century Britain.

Karl Marx (1818–83) wrote little about getting pissed, though we know from his correspondence with his father, Heinrich, that the philosopher and political theorist liked a drink. Marx Sr was not impressed by his son's taste for a drop, writing to him, 'Alas, your conduct has consisted merely in disorder, meandering in all the fields of knowledge, musty traditions by sombre lamplight ... with a beer glass [in hand]'.[78]

St Thomas Aquinas (1225–74) took a less disapproving line on getting hammered: 'Every sin has a corresponding contrary ... thus timidity is opposed to daring ... But no sin is opposite to drunkenness. Therefore, drunkenness is not a sin'.[32] To this syllogism, we can only respond with 'cheers!' or 'bottoms up!'

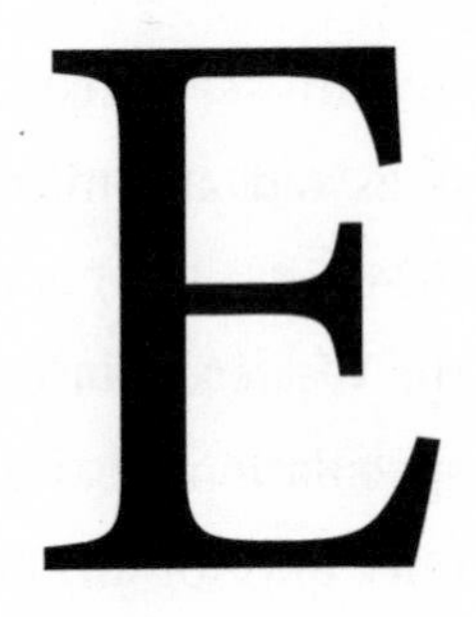

ENGLISH, the

It takes one to know one, and John Stuart Mill (1806–73) said of his compatriots, 'The English are certainly a remarkably stupid people'.[79] Well, I think the same can be said for other peoples as well.

ENTREPRENEURS (ECONOMIC)

Bertrand Russell famously wrote that 'there is much pleasure to be gained from useless knowledge'.[80] But many people – *Daily Mail* readers and those in charge of central government budgets – may be less inclined to foot the bill for philosophical pondering. What do philosophers know? Why are they wasting their time thinking about the existence of the external world, whether we are awake when we dream, and asleep when we think we are awake, and so on?

This scepticism as to the 'uselessness' of philosophy is as old as philosophising itself. Thales of Miletus (624–548 BCE) is regarded as the first philosopher of the Western world. He was much criticised for his idle speculation. So, he decided to prove his critics wrong once and for all. This is how the story was recounted by Aristotle:

> Thales, so the story goes, because he was poor, was taunted by the uselessness of philosophy; but from his insights into astronomy he had observed while it was still winter that there was going to be a large crop of olives, so he raised a small sum of money and paid round deposits for the whole of the olive-presses in Miletus and Chois, which he hired at a low rent as nobody had reason to think that it would be a bumper harvest; and when the season arrived, there was a sudden demand for a number of presses at the same time, and by letting them out on what terms he liked he realized a large sum of money, so proving that it is easy for thinkers to be rich if they choose, but this is not what

> they care about. Thales then is reported to have thus displayed his intelligence, but as a matter of fact, this device of taking an opportunity to secure a monopoly is a universal principle of business; therefore even some states have recourse to this plan as a method of raising revenue when short of funds: they introduce a monopoly of marketable goods.[81]

Generally, it is a myth that philosophers do not know how to make money. It is just that most of them find more important pursuits than growing their bank account. Voltaire, who is perhaps best known for *Candide* and the *Dictionnaire philosophique*, was – thanks to a generous loan from Tsarina Catherine the Great (1729–96) – able to set up a profitable watch-making business. The entrepreneurial philosopher boasted in a letter:

> I have set up in the hamlet of Ferney a little annex to the watchmaking industry of Bourg-en-Bresse. Our theatre … has been transformed into work-shops. There, where formerly we recited verse,

> we are now melting gold and polishing cogs. We must build new dwellings for the emigrants ... Everyone nowadays wants a gold watch, from Beijing to Martinique ... Sensitive souls will be pleased to learn that sixty Huguenots live so well with my parishioners that it is impossible to guess that there are two religions here.[82]

And, for those who consider philosophy a waste of valuable time, it is worth noting that some of the world's richest investors have studied, you guessed it, philosophy. George Soros (b. 1930), who enrolled in the philosophy programme at the London School of Economics, originally wanted to become a thinker, like Kant, Aristotle or his tutor Karl Popper (1902–94). 'I have developed a conceptual framework which has helped me [...] to make money as a hedge fund manager [...] But the framework itself is not about money, it is about the relationship between thinking and reality, a subject that has been extensively studied by philosophers from early on.'

So, just like for Thales, philosophy gave Soros 'an edge, first as a securities analyst and then as a hedge fund manager.' He decided to 'abandon [his] philosophical explorations and to focus on making money'.[83] Thales, by contrast, proved his point and then went back to pondering. Maybe he will be remembered longer than the billionaire for this very reason.

EXCREMENT

'Shitting' was the word Elizabeth Anscombe used. She famously included the term in a lecture on intrinsic pleasures, while poshly pronouncing the crisp double 't'.[84] She was not the only great mind to ponder, well, shit. Plato believed that everything had an inner 'whatness', which he called the 'form'. Everything we find in life – such as horses, goodness, love or apples – has a 'form' counterpart of a higher, almost divine order. That is, the true, perfect apple. When we behold an apple, we subconsciously compare it with the true 'form' which exists only in heaven, and we judge it according to how much likeness there is between this real apple in our hand and the one that is in heaven.

But towards the end of his life, Plato began to question this earlier view of the world, and his interlocutor Socrates found it hard to define the whatness

– or *form* – of crap, or 'mud, shit or anything totally undignified'.[85] Basically, it is hard to think of the true heavenly turd.

Aristotle took a more practical view and described how the government of Athens had made provisions 'against any dung-collector throwing down his manure near the wall [of the city]'.[86] But Aristotle – famous as the founder of biology (and practically all other academic disciplines) – also considered excrement in a more scientific way, concluding, 'either there ought to be no shit in the body or else the body ought to be able to get rid of it as soon as possible. That means, it must be in a condition that it can reject the shit as soon as it receives it for that which remains stationary – standing water for example – and that which putrefies creates disease.'[65] Whether these ponderings could be described as 'deep shit', or utter crap, is for the reader to decide.

Other philosophers have pondered the nature of excrement in a more theological vein. Pious Martin Luther thought constantly about sin, Jesus and salvation. Yet, unlike most firebrand preachers, Luther frequently used the German word *Scheiße*. The earthy former friar and founder of Lutherism, which in turn influenced the development of Protestantism, wrote of himself that he was 'ripe with shit' and even penned a rather rude sermon in which he addressed the Devil in no uncertain terms: 'Get lost, Satan, eat your own shit.'[87]

This profanity was widely used during the Middle Ages and Renaissance – as it still is now. Though some were more matter of fact in their use. For example, Montaigne wrote – correctly, we might add – 'that Kings and philosophers shit – and so do ladies have to take a dump too'.[42]

Compared to those straight-talking days, modern philosophers – with the exception of Elizabeth Anscombe – have tended to be rather restrained in their use of profanity. Though Wittgenstein, advising his fellow philosophers against pomposity, reportedly said: 'Don't try and shit higher than your arse.'[88]

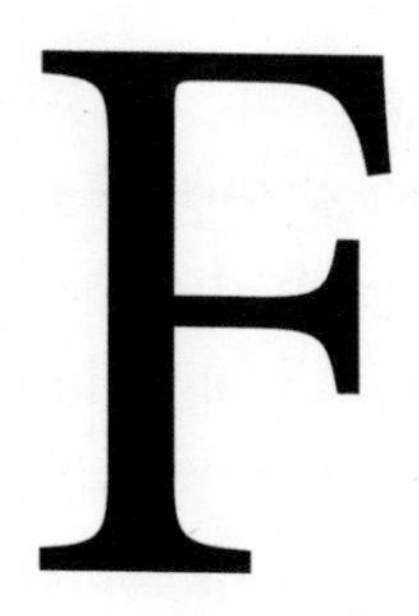

FARTING

From excretion we move on, naturally, to a related subject: the passing of wind. A person passes wind on average 15–20 times a day, concluded a study entitled, 'Investigation of normal flatus production in healthy volunteers', which was published in the appropriately named scientific journal *Gut.*[89] Always a favourite subject among naughty schoolchildren and, as it turns out, philosophers too. Perhaps many of them were more puerile than we might like to believe (see: CHILDREN). Socrates is known as the father of Western philosophy. Yet the two most famous accounts of the great man were written many years after his death by, respectively, Plato – who made him a sage – and Xenophon (431–354 BCE) – who portrayed him as a brave warrior. The only person to write about Socrates during his lifetime was rather less reverent. The playwright Aristophanes (445–385 BCE) wrote that the great man liked to fart: 'needing to take a crap, [he] would not have to spill it on his cloak [but could] satisfy his requirement by letting off a few farts'.[90]

Passing wind, was – according to this contemporaneous account – characteristic for the philosopher. In another of Aristophanes's surviving works, *The Clouds,* his character of Socrates ponders meteorological questions by way of reflections on flatulence. 'So, think about it – if your small gut can make a fart like that, why can't the air, which goes on for ever, produce tremendous thunder.'[91]

Plato himself even touched upon this subject, taking a typically more high-brow tone to note that we need remedies against farts; we 'need medicine, not just where there are injuries or seasonal illness, but … when people are full of discharges and wind like emissions from the swamp', what some are 'compelled to identify … with names such as "flatulence" or "catarrh"'.[5]

Around the same time, Diogenes was also philosophising through farts. When asked what he thought of Plato's famous Theory of Forms, he reportedly let rip a fart in response.

Much of what we know about Diogenes, as it happens, comes from Metrocles (350–280 BCE). This one-time student of Aristotle once farted while practising a speech. He reportedly got so upset that he locked himself away and considered suicide. However, a friend, Crates, went to his house and prepared a dish of lupini beans. These made him fart all the more. Metrocles realised that flatulence was natural and returned to public life, going on to write mainly about Diogenes – a famous farter! Perhaps this was not a coincidence.

Crates was an educated man, and he might have gained his knowledge about flatulence from none other than Hippocrates (460–370 BCE) – the founder of the science of medicine. The physician had written on the subject, in a scientific fashion, of course: 'All pulses produce flatulence … The lupin is the least injurious of the pulses'.[92] Incidentally, Montaigne, writing over a thousand years later, concluded, 'I know from experience that radishes are windy'.[42]

Aristotle, who wrote about everything, also touched upon this subject and defined it thus: 'farting is breath from the lower stomach'.[65]

There was little fart-talk in the Middle Ages – which seems somewhat surprising, given their generally poor diet – but the philosophical concern about farting resumed in the eighteenth century, with Hume picking up the mantle. He, of course, was an empiricist, who abhorred speculation, and who took experience as his point of departure. So, naturally, he took this approach when considering farting. The Scottish philosopher liked his food – and had, by his own account, an 'unnatural appetite'. But, in the interests of science, he set himself to testing what would occur in the nightmare scenario of skipping one's three square meals. And ultimately counselled against it, saying that self-restraint – when he tried it – resulted in there being, 'a good deal of wind in my stomach'. However, this was not a matter that concerned him overly as it 'comes away easily'.[33]

Roughly at the same time, in 1722 to be exact, Jonathan Swift (1667–1745), well known as the author of *Gulliver's Travels*, published another book, though this time under a pseudonym. The alias rather gives the game away. It was Don Fartinando Puff-Indorst, purportedly the Professor of Bumbast at the University of Crackow, and the title of the learned study was *The Benefit of Farting Explain'd*. According to the frontispiece it was 'translated into English at the Request and for the Use of the Lady Damp-Fart, of Her-fart-shire' by 'Obadiah Fizzle, Groom of the Stool to the Princess of Arse-Mini in Sardinia'.[93] The book, it should be noted, is still in print!

FAT

In one of the Hadith – the numerous sayings attributed to the Prophet Muhammad – it is reported that the Muslim elder Umar ibn al-Khattab saw a man with a large belly and said, 'What is this?' The man said, 'It is a blessing from Allah.' Umar replied, 'No, rather it is a punishment.'[94] David Hume – who was less pious – took a different view, at least if we can infer from his physique. 'An infant becomes a man, and is sometimes fat,' he wrote.[7] Very true. Indeed, Madame Geoffrin (1699–1777), a renowned Parisian *salonnière* and intellectual who played host to the famous *philosophes* and *encyclopédistes* of the day, called Hume 'my fat wag' and 'my fat rascal', while the Earl of Charlemont (1728–99), a prominent politician of the period, described the corpulent philosopher's face as 'broad and fat'. But Hume was not one to be fat-shamed. Indeed, he was rather proud to be 'sturdy and rotund', as he put it in a letter to his physician friend George Cheyne.[95]

Montaigne, likewise, was stoical about the fact that 'with the passage of time I … have grown more fat'.[42] Maybe we should all adopt this philosophical attitude to the bulge.

Simone de Beauvoir, arguably the most important feminist philosopher ever, was not kind to her heavier sisters – nor to those who make the grave error of growing older. 'It is all very well for a young girl to be a bit plump, but it doesn't do for aging women'.[14] Fat is a feminist issue! Though, not, it seems, for the author of *The Second Sex*.

FOOD

As philosophers we must go back to first principles. No one knew this better than Simone Weil (1909–43) who urged us never to 'distinguish between what is essential and what is fortuitous', as 'Man requires not rice or potatoes, but food'.[96]

The Christian philosophers rather liked their food. St Augustine, the pleasure-loving, pear-scrumping north African Bishop of Hippo (354–430), remarked that 'Whenever a man takes more meat and drink than is necessary, he should know that this is one of the lesser sins'.[97]

Thomas Hobbes shared very little with St Augustine. They differed on ethics, religion and science, but also in their attitudes to food. The English philosopher used the noun 'food' twenty-nine times in *Leviathan*. He did *not* do so approvingly. Maybe English philosophers were just a sour lot who did not appreciate the finer things in life. Certainly, Locke, Hobbes's younger compatriot, advised that the 'diet … ought to be very plain and simple'.[70]

Søren Kierkegaard was a man of wealth and refined taste and had only scorn for those who scoffed down their food. In *Either/Or*, he wrote that 'Of all ridiculous things the most ridiculous seems to me, to be busy – to be a man who is brisk about his food'.[26]

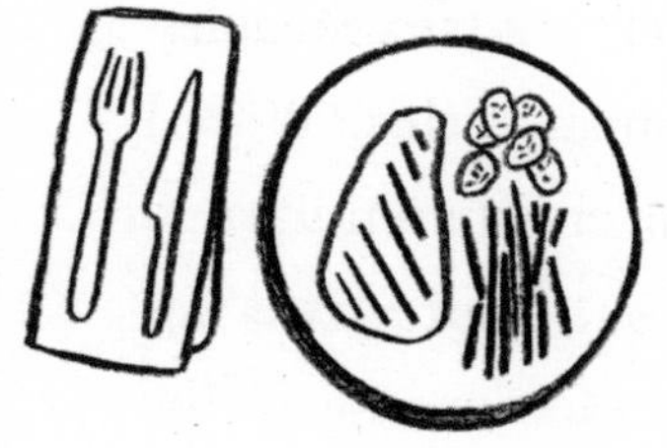

But the Danish existentialist was silent on the question of

what kinds of food he preferred to consume. Ludwig Wittgenstein was rather more direct. He abhorred extravagant meals. 'Let me be quite clear,' the Austrian told his friend Maurice Drury after a feast in the latter's house, 'while we are here, we are not going to live in this style. We will have a plate of porridge for breakfast, vegetables from the garden for lunch, and a boiled egg in the evening.'[98]

Whether Drury found Wittgenstein a more tolerable houseguest than John Maynard Keynes did (see: CHEESE) sadly goes unreported.

FOOTBALL

The existentialists Jean-Paul Sartre (1905–80) and Albert Camus (1913–60) fell out in the 1950s. There are different theories as to the cause of their disagreement – politics, women or other small matters – but few have suggested that the real cause could have been football. Albert Camus – a talented goalkeeper – famously offered the insight that 'What I know most surely in the long run about morality and obligations, I owe to football'. Jean-Paul Sartre was not so sure – hence, perhaps, their disagreement. The author of *Existentialism Is Humanism* and *No Exit* observed that 'In football everything is complicated by the presence of the other team'.[99]

It seems that existentialists had a thing for football. Martin Heidegger might be best known for his dense work *Being and Time.* But he was also passionate about *Fußball.* His biographer writes of how the great philosopher became obsessed with the game around the time when West Germany won the FIFA World Cup in 1974. By this point, Heidegger was an esteemed elderly gentleman, and his former roughness and severity had mellowed with the years. His biographer reports that he would go to the neighbours' house to watch European Cup matches on television. His particular favourite was Bayern Munich defender Franz Beckenbauer. Heidegger apparently was full of admiration for *Der Kaiser*, as Beckenbauer was known. The Bayern captain had delicate ball control, something the ageing Heidegger would demonstrate by imitating his moves. The philosopher called Beckenbauer an 'inspired player' and praised his 'invulnerability' in duels on the pitch.[100]

Franz Beckenbauer had a certain air of a thinker about him. Heidegger's appreciation of this quality may perhaps explain why the Bavarian maestro was included in the German philosophers' team that played the Greek thinkers in Monty Python's famous 1972 'Philosophers' Football Match' sketch. The Bayern Munich captain appeared alongside Hegel (played by Graham Chapman), Nietzsche (Michael Palin), Marx (Terry Jones) and Kant (Terry Gilliam). What you may not know is that Beckenbauer was on the pitch playing himself in the sketch.

Sometimes the inspiration goes the other way. Former Arsenal manager Arsène Wenger – also known as *Le Prof* for his cerebral manner – was philosophical when he spoke about '*le foot*' and concluded that different playing styles were a result of different philosophies.

> If you think about it, the culture of a country is dictated by what they learn in school. We in France have Descartes. His rationalism is the basis for all French thought and culture. In Italy you have Machiavelli, who is also about being rational and calculating.

He went on to say that 'in England, maybe because they are an island, they are more warlike'.[101]

Certainly, his take chimes with Thomas Hobbes's observation that his compatriots 'are continually in competition for honour, and consequently amongst men ariseth on that ground, envy and hatred, and finally war'.[25] So, you need to look at the whole picture.

Another football manager, José Mourinho – then the none-too-successful manager of Manchester United – was equally philosophical when he referenced Hegel's *Phenomenology of the Spirit.* After a 3 - 0 defeat to Tottenham Hotspur, the Portuguese manager asked a baffled journalist if he had 'spent [any] time reading Hegel', before going on to lecture him that 'Hegel says: "The truth is in the whole", is always in the whole'.[102]

This relationship between football and philosophy is not surprising, when you think about it. After all, as the legendary late Liverpool manager Bill Shankly reportedly observed, 'Some people believe that football is a matter of life and death … I can assure you it is much more important than that.'[103]

No wonder that the French Algerian post-structuralist Jacques Derrida claimed that he would rather have been known as an international footballer than a philosopher.[104]

GARDENING

'Let's cultivate our garden.' Thus ends Voltaire's *Candide* (1759). The eponymous hero was responding to his philosopher mentor, Dr Pangloss, who always believed that everything was the best it could possibly be 'in the best of all possible worlds'.[105] But the author of this picaresque riposte against Leibnizian optimism really was green-fingered. We know that, while living in exile from France, Voltaire enjoyed the gardens of leafy Wandsworth and Covent Garden, then on the fringes of London, and later dabbled in horticulture himself on his estates outside Geneva and at Ferney.

The remark at the end of the humorous book was not accidental but reflected the philosopher's lifelong interest in horticulture, or so experts on the subject believe.[106]

Voltaire was one in a long line of illustrious philosopher-gardeners. Going back to classical times, the Roman statesman and thinker Marcus Tullius Cicero (106–43 BCE) wrote: 'If you have a garden and a library, you have everything you need'.[107]

A love of gardening flourished – along with many other disciplines – in the Renaissance. Sir Francis Bacon is often cited for the saying that 'Gardening is the purest of human pleasures'[108] while the social philosopher and humanist Sir Thomas More (1478–1535) wrote that 'gardening gives pleasure of itself'.[109]

John Milton (1608–74) was a keen botanist before he became blind, and his garden in Aldersgate Street, London, was reportedly arranged in blending harmonies of colour throughout spring, summer and autumn. Perhaps the reason that his fine epic poem *Paradise Lost* speaks to us still is down to his instinctive understanding of what it must have been like for Adam and Eve when they were banished from 'this garden, planted with the trees of God'.[110] David Hume, by contrast, was not a practising gardener but nevertheless appreciated horticulture as an artform and described the bliss of 'walking in a garden', noting that 'the gardens, which the rich man enjoys' were both 'lively and agreeable'.[7]

Of course, the enjoyment of gardening is not the same as being good at it. Confucius (551–479 BCE) was not normally a humble man, but the Chinese sage was less confident of his own abilities when it came to the art of growing plants: 'I am not as good as an old gardener,' he admitted.[111]

GLUTTONY

Many devotional portraits, crucifixes and altarpieces suggest that Jesus was undernourished. Of course, none of the artists who created these images ever saw Jesus, or even drew on a solid account of what he really looked like. It is unlikely that he bore much resemblance to the thin man with the defined abs that we find represented in churches. If you read the Bible carefully you will appreciate this. Indeed, the Christians' Saviour – by his own admission – rather liked his food, or certainly more than his ascetic friend John the Baptist: 'For John the Baptist came neither eating bread nor drinking wine, and you say, "He has a demon!" The Son of Man has come eating and drinking, and you say, "Look at this glutton and drunkard, a friend of tax collectors and sinners!"'[112] In the ninth century, Islamic philosophy was making headway, and the first thinker to write about deeper things was al-Farabi. Often described as the first philosopher of the Islamic Golden Age, we know very little about the Baghdad-based thinker. Except that the pictures of him portray him as exceptionally lean. It perhaps stands to reason, for he wrote, 'Human beings tend to be crude, cruel, and gluttonous in stuffing themselves with food'.[113]

It seems less surprising to consider that St Thomas Aquinas was a big guy. He liked his food too. He acknowledged that by definition 'gluttony is immoderation in food'. But he was relaxed about this and, shrugging the saintly shoulders, noted that 'man cannot avoid this' – that is, overeating. In any case, it didn't matter. For Thomas concluded gluttony was 'not a sin'.[32]

Thomas Hobbes was well known for his often thinly disguised hostility towards Christianity. Given that both Jesus and Thomas Aquinas were relaxed about gluttony, it is unsurprising that Hobbes, a lifelong contrarian, took the opposite view. He believed that too much eating makes you a poor philosopher, 'the appetite of food take away the care of knowing causes', and gluttony would even make you dumb, as men who 'study nothing but their food ... are content to believe any absurdity'.[25]

Immanuel Kant was less hostile to religion than Hobbes, but no more tolerant when it came to being fat. A scrawny little man, the Prussian philosopher found that

> Brutish excess in the use of food ... is misuse of the means of nourishment that restricts or exhausts our capacity to use them intelligently. Gluttony ... is the vice that comes under this heading ... When stuffed with food a man is in a condition in which he is incapacitated, for a time, for actions that would require him to use his powers with skill and deliberation. It is obvious that putting oneself in such a state violates a duty to oneself.[114]

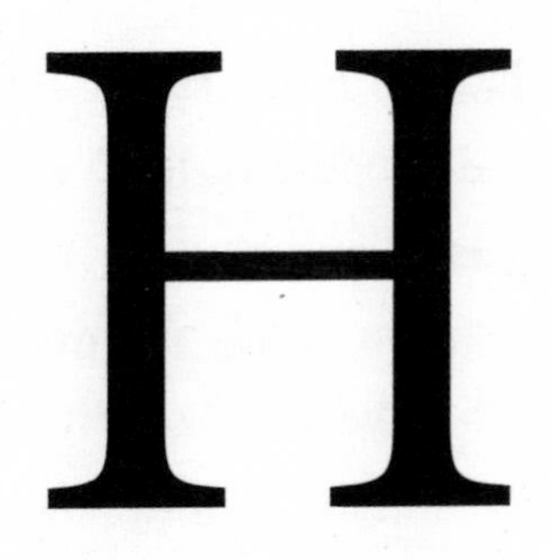

HICCUPS

Many great minds have been exercised by the mysterious causes and cures of hiccups. Plato – always one to look to first causes – believed that if 'he had eaten too much … [he] had the hiccough', though uncharacteristically he also entertained the idea that this form of synchronous diaphragmatic flutter – to use the scientific term – could 'come from some other cause'.[115]

So, maybe we should skip the causes and go straight to the possible cures. Aristotle wrote that 'heat causes concoction, hence vinegar stops hiccups … so does holding your breath if the hiccup is only slight, for it heats the breath which is constricted'. Or perhaps the way to get rid of one unwanted reflex was to fall back on another: 'sneezing stops hiccupping,' the Athenian wrote, though he added that 'it didn't stop burping'.[65]

Søren Kierkegaard would have concurred: 'He had become free from his hiccups, but not before he had come to sneeze'.[116] Kierkegaard had also thought deeply about this other activity, which he greatly enjoyed (see: SNEEZING).

But, of course, not everyone finds hiccups annoying. Lord Byron (1788–1824) rather enjoyed the sensation, or so, at least, we may deduce from a letter he wrote to a friend, 'I carried away much wine, and the wine had previously carried away my memory; so that all was hiccup and happiness for the last hour or so'.[117]

HOLIDAYS

Whether it's a five-star weekend break, a budget get-away or glamping at Glastonbury, most of us look forward to a bit of time away. Some philosophers, however, have taken a dim view of vacations. Emily Thomas, in her book *The Meaning of Travel: Philosophers Abroad*, recounts how Francis Bacon claimed that 'travel would bring about the apocalypse'.[118]

Wittgenstein, too, gave vacations a bad name when he contemptuously wrote that 'philosophical problems arise when language goes on holiday'.[10] It must have been an issue that exercised him a fair bit, for he later used an example of an exchange which suggests – as we have seen elsewhere in this book (see: FOOD and CHEESE) – that his visits were rather stressful occasions for all concerned. How else can we interpret the following? 'I am asked: "How long are you staying here?" I reply: "Tomorrow I am going away; it's the end of my holidays."'[10]

Others had happier memories. Wittgenstein's compatriot Karl Popper recalled a vacation in 1932 'in the beautiful Tyrolese hills'. 'We had,' he wrote, 'a happy time, with plenty of sunshine, and I think all tremendously enjoyed these long and fascinating talks.'[119] Of course, Popper and Wittgenstein were notoriously bitter rivals, so it is perhaps to be expected that the two also differed on the enjoyment of holidays.

Popper was not a fan of Plato, and his book *The Open Society and Its Enemies* was a long diatribe against the ancient Greek philosopher. Still, on one matter Popper and Plato agreed: they both liked holidays. The Greek wrote late in life that, 'No one was to be praised more than holiday-makers'. The person who organised vacations 'should be highly esteemed and deserves to be awarded the first prize'.[48]

Hannah Arendt would have concurred, and she also relished the relative anonymity that travel can bring. She wrote, 'Loving life is easy when you are abroad. Where no one knows your name and you hold your life in your hands all alone, you are more master of yourself than at any other time. In the opacity of foreign places all specific references to yourself are blurred'.[72]

Hans Christian Andersen (1805–75) put it equally well: 'To move, to breathe, to fly, to float, / To gain all while you give, / To roam the roads of lands remote, / To travel is to live.'[120]

HORN, the

Niccolò Machiavelli (1469–1527) has not enjoyed the greatest of reputations. *The Prince*, a cynical and at times brutal book about the necessity of doing evil in order to win power, was the reason William Shakespeare (1564–1616) called him 'the murderous Machiavel'.[121] The Italian's reputation is unlikely to be improved in your mind if you read his letters. In one letter, he confided in his friend that he was 'very horny without [his] wife' and was lured into 'the home of a washerwoman' in Lombardy while on official business. The lady in question, according to his account, was not exactly a looker.

> Her eyebrows were full of lice; one eye looked down and the other up. The corners of her eyes were full of secretion … her nose was twisted into a peculiar shape, the nostrils were full of snot and one of them was half missing. Her mouth looked like Lorenzo de Medici's, twisted on one side and dribbling since she had no teeth to keep the saliva in her mouth. Her lip was covered with a thin but rather long mustachio.

However, the Renaissance writer apparently only realised this after he had had his way with her – I will spare readers the colourful description of the washer-woman's nether regions … The philosopher 'vomited over her', and confided to the friend, 'that I will not be horny again as long as I am in Lombardy'.[122]

Friedrich Nietzsche – who had very little success with women – was so terrified and flummoxed by the whole business of sexual attraction that he pondered: 'Is it not better to be in the hands of a murderer than to be on a horny woman's mind?'[67] To which the common-sense answer is 'No, Friedrich, it is not!'

Rousseau, while on a visit to Venice, was overcome with the same desires as Machiavelli and reported that 'he entered the chamber of a woman of easy virtue, as the sanctuary of love and beauty', and that the woman in question was stunning and the lustful philosopher was taken aback by 'the clearness of her skin, the brilliancy of her complexion, her white teeth, sweet breath, and the appearance of neatness about her person'. Alas, the Italian beauty did not reciprocate his feelings, especially after he took to analysing her anatomy, and sent him away with the comment, '*lascia le donne, a studia la matematica*' – which roughly translates as, 'forget about women and go and study mathematics'.[123]

HORSES

Horses have a long philosophical pedigree. Plato used this noble animal as a prime example to describe his theory of forms. As we have seen, he believed that behind every single object there is an imaginary form – *eidos* in Greek – and that, in order to understand the world around us, we automatically compare the real things we encounter with their ideal versions. For example, we might find Red Rum – the champion steeplechaser that won the Grand National in 1973, 1974 and 1977 – to be a beautiful steed. We do so, Plato would argue, because this thoroughbred was closer to the ideal horse – or had more 'horseness' (*hippotes*, in Greek) – than the average mount. According to Plato, each actual horse was a more or less imperfect copy. The closer to the original 'form', the more beautiful it was.[124] Not everyone was convinced by this argument. Antisthenes (446–366 BCE), another of Socrates's pupils, objected: 'I can see the horse but not the horseness'.[125]

Confucius, on the other hand, opined that 'A good horse is praised for its virtue, not for its strength'.[111] Thomas Aquinas – who was euphemistically 'large' – didn't write much on these noble beasts, but he did die after falling off one.

David Hume – who did not exactly have a jockey's physique either – nevertheless was a keen horseman who made it 'a constant rule to ride twice or thrice a week'.[33] In his view, the climate was responsible for the various types of horses. Thus, 'Flanders is remarkable for large and heavy horses; Spain for horses light, and good of mettle. And any breed of these creatures transplanted from one country to another, will soon lose the qualities which they derived from their native climate.' He even suggested that the same could be true for humans: 'It may be asked why not the same with men?' He went on to remark that

> At present no part of Europe [has] so bad horses of all kinds as France; but Germany abounds with excellent horses. This may beget little suspicion that even animals depend not on the climate but on the different breeds, and on the skill and care in rearing them. The north of England abounds in the best horses of all kinds which are perhaps in the world. In the neighbouring counties, north side of the Tweed [i.e., in Hume's native Scotland] no good horses of any kind are to be met with.[126]

We should take his dismissal of French horses with a pinch of hay: it might be a consequence of his general attitude towards our neighbours across the Channel. 'Our jealousy and hatred of France are without bounds.'[126]

In any case, through the ages other writers took a different view. Julius Caesar (100–44 BCE) observed that 'the horses of Gaul were very good, whereas those in Germany very bad'.[127] David Hume – to his credit – noted this disagreement with the Roman emperor in a footnote!

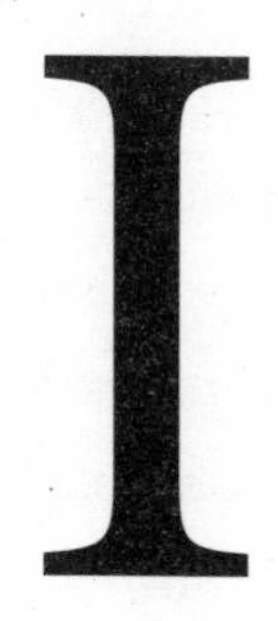

INNOCENT PLEASURES

What could possibly be wrong with innocent pleasures? Well, Kierkegaard found one objection, and a rather convincing one at that: 'As for innocent pleasures in life. Well, they suffer from one deficiency only, that they are innocent'.[26]

INSULTS

After their deaths, philosophers become revered as wise men and women who pondered the deepest questions with utmost impartiality; who did not resort to insults but focused on rational arguments. Isn't that right? Not so! Even the greatest minds belonged to sometimes petty individuals who said some rather unpleasant things about their colleagues. Søren Kierkegaard described his opponent Bishop H. L. Martensen as 'a glob of snot'.[128]

Karl Popper, promoting the scientific method, advocated the use of arguments that could be proven wrong – or 'falsified'. But when the Austrian-born philosopher wrote about Martin Heidegger, he did not follow his own prescription. 'I appeal to the philosophers of all countries to unite and never again mention Heidegger or talk to a philosopher who defends Heidegger. This man was a devil.'[129] Why was Popper so exercised? Was it because of Heidegger's antisemitism, or his Nazi Party membership? No, not quite. Popper hated his German colleague for being vague and careless with language.

Speaking of precision with language, Epicurus reportedly was none too friendly towards his rivals and had a colourful way of expressing his low opinion of them: 'Nausiphanes [of whom we know nothing] was a jellyfish, a cheat, and a whore', and 'Aristotle [was] a waste, after he spent his inheritance he sold drugs'.[130] There were no libel laws in ancient Greece. Nor in France in the seventeenth century, when René Descartes snidely opined that 'Pascal [the science genius who codified the concept of the vacuum, among other things] has too much vacuum in his brain'.[131]

J

JOKES

'In ancient time he was crowned king who could best praise the dead. In our times, he ought to be crowned who can tell the best jokes'.[26] Some would say that this could explain the election of Boris Johnson and Silvio Berlusconi. Maybe Kierkegaard knew something contemporary political scientists don't? But the existentialist philosopher's remark raises another important question. Namely, why do we joke? Sigmund Freud had an answer to everything – though not necessarily the correct one. He took a particular interest in jokes and even wrote a whole book about them, in which he concluded that '[the joke] enables the enjoyment of a drive (a lustful and hostile one) against a barrier standing in its way, it circumvents this barrier and thus draws enjoyment from a source of pleasure that has become inaccessible due to the obstacle'.[132]

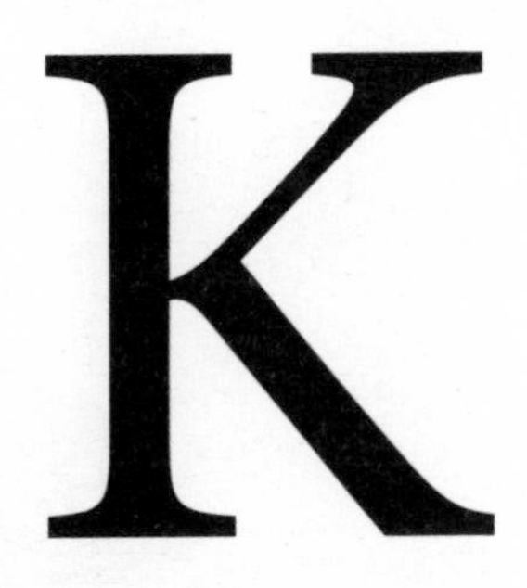

KISSING

Great philosophers, according to Hannah Arendt, 'cannot think without kisses'.[133] So, when Nietzsche wrote that the eponymous Zarathustra 'desired to be kissed', it was totally understandable.[67]

Marilyn Monroe (1926–63) was wrong when she sang that a kiss is not as good as diamonds. An avid reader – she was once spotted reading James Joyce's *Ulysses* – perhaps the film star had even read Kierkegaard, who pointed out that 'One ... makes a Difference between the first Kiss and all the others. What is reflected on here is incommensurable for what appears in the other divisions, it is indifferent to the sound, the touch, the time in general'.[26] There's nothing like your first kiss.

LAUGHTER

Epicurus was known to be a cheerful soul, and true to his *joie de vivre* approach, the Greek philosopher believed that we 'must laugh and philosophize and manage our households'.[134] Well, that neatly sums it up, doesn't it? Not exactly, for philosophers disagree almost by definition, including on why we giggle and guffaw. Henri-Louis Bergson (1859–1941), a rather serious Frenchman, devoted a – rather humourless – book to the subject, observing that 'a landscape may be beautiful, charming, and sublime, or insignificant or ugly; it will never be laughable'. For what is 'comic does not exist outside the pale of the strictly human'. Hence, 'you may laugh at an animal, but only because you have discovered in it some human attitude or expression'.[135]

Basically, when it comes to getting the giggles, there are three reasons – we might:

1. Laugh at others, but we might also,
2. Laugh when we encounter absurdities, and we might,
3. Laugh when we are faced with horrors that require the release of emotional energy

We can take them one by one. For Hobbes, laughter was a way of showing superiority: 'laughter is caused … by the apprehension of some deformed thing in another, by comparison whereof they suddenly applaud themselves'.[25]

Arendt did not disagree with Hobbes, but she thought there was more to laughter than the Englishman had argued. In her last – and most philosophical – work, *The Life of the Mind*, Arendt found that laughter was quite innocent and rather different from the ridicule that Hobbes had ascribed to it, though she too admitted that laughter could be a 'fearful weapon'.[136]

For her, a chortle was also a way of getting relief from pain. She reportedly forced herself to laugh uncontrollably when she was researching *Eichmann in Jerusalem* (1963), her celebrated book on the trial of a key Holocaust perpetrator. This approach is sometimes ascribed to the 'Relief Theory of Laughter'. The importance of a thing depends on how much we can joke about it. Hence, we make jokes in very bad taste about the most gruesome and upsetting things in order to come to terms with the unthinkable. Next time you are offended, be charitable. Consider that the person just needs a bit of literal comic relief.

Anthony Ashley Cooper, 3rd Earl of Shaftesbury (1671–1713) – whose grandfather the 1st Earl had been a patron of John Locke – was the first writer to write about this view of laughter. In 1709 he mused that

> The natural free spirits of ingenious men [and women], if imprisoned or controlled, will find out other ways of motion to relieve themselves in their constraint; and whether it be in burlesque, mimicry, or buffoonery, they will be glad at any rate to vent themselves, and be revenged upon their constrainers.[137]

Other writers have taken a different view on the causes of laughter. Kant is normally known for his dense and forbidding style, yet he was unusually clear and to the point when he observed that

> In everything that is to excite a lively convulsive laugh there must be something absurd (in which the understanding, therefore, can find no satisfaction). Laughter is an affection arising from the sudden transformation of a strained expectation into nothing.[138]

Those who like labels have called this the 'Incongruity Theory of Laughter'.

But not all philosophers have been convinced of the benefits of laughter. Old stick-in-the-mud Plato recommended that the guardians of his ideal state should not be 'too fond of laughter'.[5] And that is no laughing matter!

LAZINESS

Paul Lafargue (1842–1911), the Caribbean journalist who married Karl Marx's daughter Laura, was a remarkable man. Born in Cuba to French and Creole parents, he spent most of his adult life in France, though with shorter stints in England and Spain. At the age of sixty-nine, he and sixty-six-year-old Laura died together in a suicide pact. But the reason we include him here is that he wrote a book with the interesting title *The Right to Be Lazy.* He began the book with a battle cry for idleness.

> A strange delusion possesses the working classes of the nations where capitalist civilization holds its sway. This misconception drags in its train the individual and social miseries which for two centuries have tormented sad humanity. This delusion is the love of work, the furious passion for work, pushed even to the exhaustion of the vital force of the individual and his progeny. Instead of opposing this mental abnormality, the clerics, the economists, and the moralists have cast a sacred halo over work.[139]

Gotthold Ephraim Lessing (1729–81) was a very respected thinker and poet. However, when he faced an essay crisis as a twenty-two-year-old student, he decided that be couldn't be bothered, and instead of concentrating on Latin verbs, he wrote an ode to laziness: 'Let us be lazy in everything, except in loving and drinking, except in being lazy'.[140] In 1784, after Lessing's death, the composer Joseph Haydn (1732–1809) set the poem to music.[141]

Lessing's was not a popular view among all thinkers, especially men of the cloth. Bishop George Berkeley was an able – and we must assume hard-working – philosopher who believed that 'the Lord conceal(s) Himself from the eyes of … the lazy'.[3] Thomas Aquinas believed that laziness – or 'Sloth' as he called it – denotes 'sorrow for spiritual good', The philosophical friar concluded that 'it is evil … on two counts, both in itself and in point of its effect'.[32]

On the other hand, Bertrand Russell delighted in being in opposition to Christian thinkers. This may explain why he authored a book with the telling title *In Praise of Idleness*, where he – to cut a long story short – found that laziness is productive.

As much as Russell believed that his book was pathbreaking and innovative, it was in fact following in the footsteps of earlier writers, including some of the ancient Greeks who were fond of laziness – even if they did not practise what they preached. Aristotle did not exactly idle his life away, and yet, he wrote, 'leisure seems itself to contain pleasure and happiness and felicity of life. And this is not possessed by the busy but by the leisured'.[81] Or, as the German romantic writer Friedrich von Schlegel (1772–1829) is often quoted as saying, 'Laziness is the one divine fragment of a godlike existence left to man from paradise.' Whether he actually said this is questionable. But the sentiment was not foreign to other philosophers. Montaigne – who was busy writing one of the longest books in the canon of Western thought – nevertheless believed that 'the greatest favour I could do for my mind was to leave it in complete sluggishness, caring for itself, concerned only with itself, serenely thinking of itself'. Though he admitted that this 'idleness produces erratic changes of the mind'.[42]

But overall, philosophers and other great minds have taken a dim view of indolence and inactivity. 'Laziness is the mother of all evil,' Solon (630–560 BCE), a statesman who laid the foundations of ancient Athenian democracy, is said to have claimed.

This seems rather unfair. As the old joke goes, don't blame the lazy, they didn't do anything!

LISTENING

Are you paying attention? Philosophers are a verbose lot. Most of them, it is fair to say, prefer to speak rather than to listen. But, just sometimes, they are humble and come to their senses.

Søren Kierkegaard, though he too wrote a lot, confessed he had 'less and less to say … became silent, and began to listen', and at this stage, 'discovered in the silence the voice of God'.[142] For the Danish existentialist, listening opened the door to a spiritual awakening.

But what does it mean to listen? Fundamentally, we need to understand that 'hearing', in the words of Roland Barthes, 'is a physiological phenomenon. Listening is a psychological act'.[143] Listening, therefore, is a social phenomenon in a way that mere hearing is not.

The art of listening is as old as philosophy itself, but it is something people have always found difficult. 'Good words scarcely find any listeners,' wrote St Augustine of Hippo.[144] There is a serious point here. For, in not hearing others out, we deprive ourselves of the insight of our fellow citizens. That is what the medieval philosopher Marsilius of Padua (1275–1342) realised when he urged those in power to listen. For, 'the less learned citizen can sometimes perceive something that should be corrected regarding a proposed law even if they would not have known how to ascertain it in the first place'.[145] Whether profound or not, it is worth noting that the word 'listen' is an anagram of the word 'silent'.

LOVE

John Stuart Mill may not have looked like a heartthrob or a romantic lover. But whatever we look like, we all – I hope – fall in love. And many of us who do might wish that we had the gift for writing that Mill possessed. For he was not just an eloquent essayist who could explain the meaning of freedom, political economy or abstract logic. No, Mill was also a man who was able to express his deepest feelings. Just consider these lines from his diary:

> What a sense of protection is given by the consciousness of being loved, and what an additional sense, over and above this, by being

> near the one by whom one is and wishes to be loved the best. I have experience at present of both these things; for I feel as if no really dangerous illness could actually happen to me while I have her care for me; and yet I feel as if by coming away from her I had parted with a kind of talisman, and I was more open to attacks of the enemy than while I was with her.[146]

Mill and Harriet Taylor Mill had been married three years when he wrote these lines. Surprisingly, not many philosophers have written about love. Perhaps this feeling does not lend itself to rational analysis. But there are exceptions, of course. Plato is one.

In *Symposium* (*c.* 385–370 BCE) he observed that, 'Love was the greatest among the gods, and that humans and God alike marvel at Eros'. Getting more to the point, he continued, 'Personally I cannot think that a man can have any greater blessing than an honourable lover.'[115] In the same passage, he made it clear that this lover should be male.

What the best philosophers can muster on the subject is usually found in their private correspondence, such as the letters exchanged between Heidegger and Arendt. These letters were so full of longing, tenderness and passion that they became pure poetry. 'I kiss you on the forehead and your eyes,' Arendt wrote to Heidegger, who – in many more lovestruck letters – responded by calling her *meine Liebste,* 'my most beloved'.[147]

When you are in love even the most mundane and banal everyday tasks become lighter, and you float away on a breeze of joy. Hannah Arendt – unlike Heidegger – was a pro when it came to writing about love. Indeed, she gained a doctorate on the unlikely subject of St Augustine and the concept of love, entitling her dissertation *Love and Saint Augustine* – although the Catholic saint himself wrote precious little on the subject.[148] Around the time when she was writing her dissertation, José Ortega y Gasset (1883–1955) published his *Estudios sobre el Amor* – or *On Love: Aspects of a Single Theme*, as the title is usually translated. However, some of the rather impenetrable lines in this book – such as 'love is that splendid triggering of human vitality, which nature affords anyone for going out of himself'[149] – raise the question of whether the Spaniard had ever actually been infatuated with another human being. On the basis of this quote, one would think the answer is negative.

M

MAKE-UP

While Simone de Beauvoir habitually sported a slash of red lipstick,[14] it is to a more surprising source, Bertrand Russell, whom we must turn for a philosophical consideration of the problem: 'Who may use lipstick?' This lesser-known paper – admittedly not his most difficult piece and certainly an easier read than *Principia Mathematica* – nevertheless raises important questions. For example, why was it that all women save for a few professions were allowed to wear lipstick? According to Russell, it was a commonly held view that 'welfare workers should not employ lipstick, in spite of the fact that all the ladies from whom their funds come do so'. After chewing over this hypocrisy for some time, Russell eventually concluded that in fact, *all* women should wear lipstick, as this showed that they were jolly, which he took to be a good thing.[57] Nowadays, we may find his reasoning more than a little dubious, and feel he might as well have posed the question: why are eyeshadow, lipstick and mascara never mad at each other? (Answer: because they always make up!)

MARRIAGE

The caricature of the otherworldly philosopher is often that of the absent-minded bachelor. And certainly, a fair number of them fall into the 'single man' category. Ludwig Wittgenstein, Thomas Aquinas, John Locke, Benedict Spinoza and Friedrich Nietzsche have very little in common, except that they remained unmarried.

Of course, there were numerous exceptions, including Hegel, Marx and Aristotle. Plato, who also had a spouse, adopted a rather unforgiving view of those who avoided nuptials. His aforementioned colleagues would have suffered severe consequences under the Athenian's dream regime. In *Laws*, he spoke about 'the obligation to marry', saying 'if anyone disobeys [this duty], and unsocially keeps himself to himself so that he is still unmarried at the age of thirty-five, he must pay an annual fine'.[48]

Immanuel Kant, although another bachelor, nevertheless reflected on aspects of the institution of marriage. The Prussian – and if this was his idea of romance, we can see why he never got hitched – defined marriage as the monopoly of the use of the partner's genitals and as 'the reciprocal use that one human being makes of the sexual organs and capacities of another…'[114]

Thomas Aquinas – also rather lacking in first-hand experience – was less creative in his reflections on the subject, since he was at pains not to depart from the Church line. He wrote: 'In matrimony there is a joining in respect of which we speak of husband and wife; and this joining, through being directed to some one thing [procreation], is matrimony; while the joining together of bodies and minds is a result of matrimony.'[32]

Few could be further apart than Thomas Aquinas and his namesake Thomas Hobbes on many topics, including marriage. The bachelor Hobbes took a dim view of matrimony. This was expressed in the section on 'Eternal Torment' in his most famous book, *Leviathan*. 'For the wicked,' he wrote, 'may marry, and give in marriage, and have grosse and corruptible

bodies, as all mankind now have'.[25] No spiritual union of bodies and minds here. Was it sour grapes?

Søren Kierkegaard, who notoriously and painfully broke off an engagement with Regine Olsen in order to devote himself to the life of a celibate philosopher, not surprisingly also pondered the institution of matrimony. True to the soul-searching that characterises the father of existentialism, he wrote in *Either/Or*: 'If you marry, you will regret it; if you do not marry, you will also regret it; if you marry or if you do not marry, you will regret both; whether you marry or you do not marry, you will regret both.'[26] Well, not much guidance there. Spouses: can't live with them, can't live without them.

MONEY

David Hume was a rather matter-of-fact sort of guy. When he wrote about money, he was certainly more descriptive than prescriptive. 'Money', he dryly observed, was 'but only the instrument which men have agreed upon to facilitate the exchange of one commodity for another', or, more poetically, 'the oil which renders the motions of the wheels [of trade and commerce] more smooth and easy'.[126] Hume was relaxed about making money.

The ancient philosophers were not. In fact, they were very concerned about money-making, and getting filthy rich. Plato, in particular, was – if we can use modern terms – rather anti-capitalist and maintained that 'no private person should be allowed to possess gold or silver, but only coinage for day-to-day dealings'.[48]

In this Aristotle followed his one-time master, taking an equally dim view of money. But, as always, his style was different. The sage made a distinction between *oeconomica* (the art of running a household) and *chrematistics* (the art of wealth-making). While Aristotle admitted that money-making could be legitimate in a state, he was opposed to any form of greed, and concluded that, 'it appears necessary that there should be a limit to all riches'.[81] For, ultimately, 'money was brought into being for the purpose of exchange'. So, money, was not, according to Aristotle, an end in itself.

In the Middle Ages, Thomas Aquinas merely updated Aristotle's position, though the Italian clergyman came over more radical. He warned against 'a few rich men who take advantage of their wealth and oppress the people' and even went so far as to argue that 'men should not hold material things as their own but to the common benefit; each readily sharing them with others in their necessity'.[32] Aquinas, though a broad-minded thinker who was willing and able to quote Jewish and Muslim thinkers, did not know Confucius. But, on the matter of money, they would have been in agreement. 'It is shameful to make salary your sole object,' the Chinese sage reportedly said.[111]

This rather restrictive view of wealth is, of course, very different from that espoused by economic libertarians like the American Robert Nozick, who, in a nice turn of phrase, defended all 'Capitalist acts between consenting adults'.[13]

So, what are the consequences of the love of money? Hegel perhaps offers a fitting and prescient synthesis between the antithetical views of those who want restrictions and those who do not. In 1820, he wrote, 'the differing incentives … may collide, and while the right relation between them overall comes about automatically, still its fine-tuning requires a control that stands above both.'[150] Without state intervention in the economy, massive inequality would ensue, since capitalism brings with it 'conditions which greatly enable the concentration of unequal wealth in a few hands ... The outcome is the creation of a proletariat of the destitute.'[150] No wonder, really, that Karl Marx 'openly avowed' himself to be a 'student of that mighty thinker',[151] for, in many ways, Hegel was the more passionate and eloquent in his critique of capitalism.

NAKEDNESS

It caused a sensation when the high-brow French news magazine *Le Nouvel Observateur* published naked photos of Simone de Beauvoir on what would have been her hundredth birthday. Some, especially feminists, found it shocking that the icon of sisterhood had posed for nudes. The philosopher herself would have taken another view, however. 'Here people are a little backward. They don't understand why I go naked with a gold bracelet on my thigh' runs a line in *The Second Sex*.[152]

So, maybe other philosophers were just 'backward'. Hegel was certainly shocked by those who chose to wear nothing but their birthday suits, especially if they came from other cultures.

'Naked Fakirs wander about without any occupation,' he wrote dismissively in a disquisition on India, though he was quite certain that the Brahmins of that country 'in bathing were never totally naked'.[18]

In truth, on this topic Hegel knew only what he was told. Travelling to far-flung destinations was not the prerogative of the great minds before well into the twentieth century. So, Hegel's description may not have been based on anything as inconvenient as first-hand knowledge, or even truthful evidence.

Thomas Aquinas, some five centuries earlier, was more relaxed about nakedness. Not an attitude you might normally associate with a man who had heeded the call of the Church. But he was hardly prudish – in fact, the medieval theologian was rather liberal on some matters. He opined that 'man has a natural right to go naked because nature not having provided him with clothing, he has had to fashion it for himself'.[32]

Other thinkers and writers understood nakedness as a metaphor – for man's fundamental nature, for his hubris. The closing lines in Hans Christian Andersen's perceptive fairy tale run:

> 'But he hasn't got anything on,' a little child said. 'Did you ever hear such innocent prattle?'

said its father. And one person whispered to another what the child had said, 'He hasn't anything on. A child says he hasn't anything on.' 'But he hasn't got anything on!' the whole town cried out at last. The Emperor shivered, for he suspected they were right. But he thought, 'This procession has got to go on.' So he walked more proudly than ever.[153]

NOISE

Wittgenstein studied natural sciences before becoming a philosopher. And he never lost the fascination with this subject. But it is debatable as to whether he was as informed as he would have liked us to believe. He said, 'You can ask "was that thunder or gunfire?" Here you could not ask "was that a noise"'.[98] Well, actually, physicists have a pretty good definition of 'noise'. No less a mind than Galileo Galilei (1564–1642) wrote that noises are 'sounds heard by us when the air is ruffled'.[154] Which is perfectly clear. Likewise, Spinoza made a distinction in *Ethics* between different sounds: 'Whatsoever affects our ears is said to give rise to noise, sound, or harmony.'[53]

So, Wittgenstein: go back and read the classics before you make such silly pronouncements!

ODOUR

Philosophers nowadays are mainly concerned with abstract matters – 'being', 'essence', 'meaning' and suchlike. Back in the day, they were concerned with really important matters like why some things stink. Epicurus had an explanation: 'In the case of smell … nothing would ever produce this reaction except those certain atomic masses that move off the object and are suited to activating the sense organs,' he wrote.[155] Not bad for a guy who lived 2,200 years before the advent of quantum physics!

ORDERING FOOD

Ludwig Wittgenstein – judging by the few existing photos of the philosopher – was a very thin man. Maybe, we can but speculate, there was a reason for his slender appearance. For he spent considerable time pondering the meaning of ordering food. 'When I say that the orders "Bring me sugar" and "Bring me milk" make sense, but not the combination "Milk me sugar", that does not mean that the utterance of this combination of words has no effect'.[10] If he had just got on with ordering a coffee, and perhaps a sandwich to go with it, he might not have been quite so lean.

P

PENIS, the

On this matter, we might want to take a historical overview before we get into its, ahem, meatier aspects. Montaigne is a good starting point. The essayist tells us that the Romans 'wiped their dicks with fragrant wool after they had a go with them'.[42] This piece of information justifies – or, at least, explains – the words of the Roman poet Martial (38–104): 'I will have nothing to do with you until you have washed your tool in wool'.[156]

From Plato to de Beauvoir, the history of the philosophy of penises is bookended by writers who were in no doubt as to what men used for brains. Plato believed that the 'male genitals are unruly and self-willed, like an animal that is not subject to reason'.[157] Simone de Beauvoir concurred, writing in *The Second Sex* that

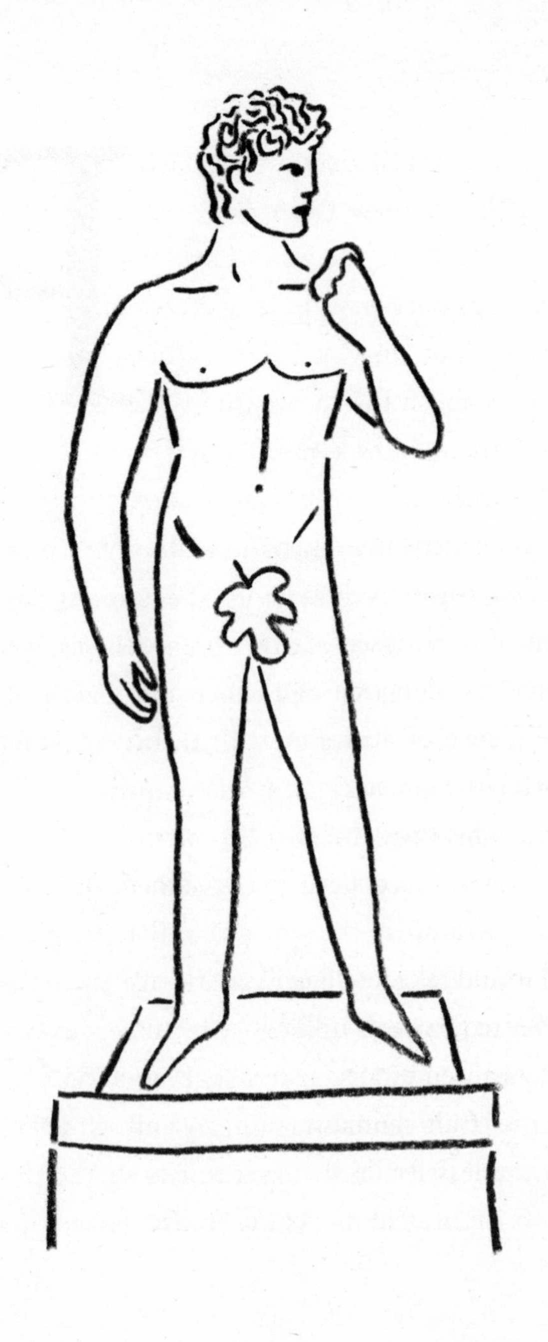

'Male eroticism is definitely located in the penis'.[152] But neither of these two wrote as extensively on the topic as Aristotle. He was a curious person – and a meticulous one. First, he would set out what he was talking about (in Greek *hoti*, 'what'), and then he would establish the causes (the Greek word for this, if you care to know, is *dioti*, 'why').

So, when the great man wanted to understand why some men fathered more children than others, he naturally began by describing various forms of sexual relations, and observed that 'fish copulate throwing themselves alongside of the females, and that men and all such creatures must hold their breath before emitting the semen'.[158]

But why, then, did some have more offspring than others? Aristotle believed it had something to do with the temperature of the semen, and that if the 'seminal fluid would take too long in its passage and be cooled' the intercourse was unlikely to result in a pregnancy. Always an empiricist, Aristotle even added his own example from humans: 'if the penis is large, such men are less fertile than when it is smaller because the semen, if cold, is not generative, and that which is carried too far is cooled'.[158] Aristotle, it might be added, begat only one son and one daughter. I leave you to draw your own conclusions.

PILL-POPPING

As far back as the 1640s, Thomas Hobbes – who reportedly was something of a hypochondriac – took the view that 'wholesome pills for the sick, which are swallowed whole, have the virtue to cure, but chewed, are for the most part cast up again without much effect'.[25] Whether this is in line with present-day pharmacokinetic thinking (the science of the interactions of the body and medicines) is debatable.

You might tend to think that philosophers just accept their lot in life – 'Sorrow is knowledge, those who need the most must mourn the deepest o'er the fatal truth, the tree of knowledge is not that of life', as Lord Byron put it.[159] But, oh no, they took pills too.

David Hume was, if not on Prozac, then at least the eighteenth-century equivalent. He took drugs against 'the lowness of spirit', and 'went under a course of bitters and anti-hysterical pills'. It seems that this regimen helped, for the effect was 'the abating of symptoms'.[33] Sigmund Freud was another great believer in taking substances to relieve symptoms. One of the psychoanalyst's first published books bore the title *Über Coca – On Cocaine.*

PLAY

We tend to think of ancient Athens as the august seat of learning, birthplace of democracy and Western culture; but for the Athenians, it was all child's play. *Paidia*, the Greek for childish play or amusement, formed the root of their word for education – *paideia*. And as if to hammer home the point, their word for leisure was *skholē* – from which our word 'school' derives. No surprise, then, that Plato, through his mouthpiece Socrates, was adamant that the best way of teaching was through play: 'the instruction must not be given the aspect of a compulsion to learn'. He went on, 'don't … use force when teaching the children but rather use play. In that way you can better determine what each is naturally directed toward.'[5]

Fast-forward almost two thousand years, and John Locke was on to the same idea: 'I have always had a fancy, that learning might be made a play and recreation to children; and that they might be brought to desire to be taught'.[70]

And, half a century later, Jean-Jacques Rousseau made a similar case for play, noting that 'every village boy of twelve knows how to use a lever better than the cleverest mechanician in the academy' because they learned it through play. 'The lessons you learn in the playground are worth a hundredfold more than what they learn in the classroom'.[160]

Rousseau, Locke and Plato were chiefly concerned with the education and behaviour of children. Aristotle went a step further and stressed that childish play was important for adults, 'for a man who is at work needs leisure, and this is the object of play, while work is accompanied by toil and exertion'.[81] It's almost as if the history of philosophy is a succession of thoughts on the benefits of playing and being childish. Nietzsche believed that the aim of life was to become a playful child, for 'he who had been lost to the world now conquers his own world through play'.[67]

In more recent times these ideas about play were taken over by psychologists. Freud found play to be a key to creativity for children as well as for adults. The father of psychoanalysis believed that 'the creative writer' 'is the same as the child at play. He creates a world of fantasy which he takes very seriously'.[161]

Of course, there are some spoil-sports who are less inclined to see play in a positive light. St Augustine could see no advantage in innocent childish playing around. He wrote approvingly that he was punished with a beating 'because, by playing with a ball, I made less progress in studies'.[162] And yet the Bishop of Hippo must have known that Scripture teaches, 'Except ye be converted, and … become as little children, ye shall not enter into the kingdom of heaven.'[163]

QUICHE

In 1992, the legal philosopher and University of Miami law professor Marc A. Fajer (b. 1961) published a paper pondering the question 'Can Two Real Men Eat Quiche Together?' To which his answer, 'real' – or 'unreal' – men may be reassured to learn, is affirmative.[164] The apparently baffling reference to the famed French savoury custard tart stems from a book, published ten years earlier, entitled *Real Men Don't Eat Quiche* by Bruce Feirstein, which – tongue-not-too-far-from-cheek – satirised the gender stereotypes of the Ronald Reagan era.

The oven-baked delicacy became part of the incipient culture wars to the extent that it was even referenced by the left-wing intellectual Noam Chomsky (b. 1928), who allegedly said that the liberal elite drink French wine and eat quiche – which, the leftist linguist apparently took as a good thing!

QUIET

Thomas Aquinas wrote a lot, but he was also aware that 'Wisdom and prudence are acquired … by one who is content to sit down and be quiet'.[32] John Stuart Mill – who was philosophically rather different from St Thomas – perhaps agreed with this sentiment when he told a gathering, 'There is nothing which I have to say, or think, that it is useful to say on this subject.'[165] So, he decided to stay quiet. There is much to be said for being quiet, but some have taken it too far. For example, it seems a slight exaggeration when Blaise Pascal (1623–62) opined that 'all of humanity's problems stem from man's inability to sit quietly'.[166]

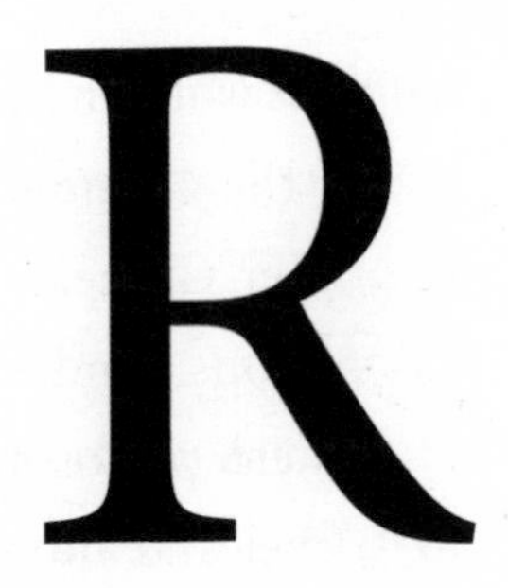

RADISHES

'At first, *radishes* agreed with my [digestion]; then they did not; now they are [once more] agreeable,' wrote Montaigne in his essay 'Of Experiences'[42] (see: FARTING). That was one view. Others had different uses for the little vegetable. In a poem addressed to his male lover, the Roman erotic poet Gaius Valerius Catullus (84–54 BCE) wrote, 'Of him whom, with feet dragged apart, an open door, radishes and mullets pass through'.[167]

ROADS

We do not know why, but the Chinese sage Laozi objected to roads as unnatural and, it is reported, 'in his disgust at such mechanistic devices, he left China to live among the Western barbarians'.[168] We cannot help but wonder whether, when departing for foreign lands, the Chinese master travelled by road… Like the other Chinese masters, he did not elaborate on the reasons. And, maybe, that is a general tendency in Eastern philosophy. The master's words are taken as gospel and no argument is needed. Perhaps this is the fundamental difference between European and Asian philosophy?

S

SEX

We all know the term 'platonic relationship', which is, in essence, an amorous bond without sex. Since the concept bears his name, it would be quite natural to believe that Plato was in favour of such chaste affairs. On the contrary. 'Can you name a pleasure greater and more exhilarating than sex?' he asked rhetorically, and immediately supplied his answer: 'I can't.'[5]

Plato wrote a fair bit on this subject. Even the gods, he wrote, could be overcome by passion, and to such a degree that they would forget everything else. 'Zeus, in a moment through his lust, was so completely overcome at the sight of Hera [his wife] that he would not even go into the hut, but wanted to lie with her on the ground, declaring he has never been in such a state of rapture before, even when they first met one another'.[169]

Overwhelming desire is not only the preserve of the deities. Sex, according to the Russian-born libertarian Ayn Rand (1905–82), 'was impervious to reason', and in her view it mocked the power of all philosophers. Being a bit of a 'goer' herself, Rand believed that person's sexual choice was the result of their fundamental convictions. Roughly speaking, her position was: tell me whom you sleep with, and I will tell you who you are and what you believe in.[170]

Immanuel Kant, while arguably a greater philosopher, was markedly less profound on this topic. He famously formulated the Categorical Imperative. This forbidding term was Kant's shorthand for always comparing our actions with higher moral principles. One of the 'imperatives' in his book was that you should never treat another person 'merely as a means to an end'.[114]

So, what does this mean in practice when we talk about sex? The Prussian took a dim view of human sexual relations and believed that, in practice, we always do treat others as a mere means to an end.

> Sexual love … taken by itself is a degradation of human nature; for as soon as a person becomes

> an object of appetite for another, all motives of moral relationship cease to function, because as an object of appetite for another a person becomes a thing and can be treated and used as such by everyone. This is the only case in which a human being is designed by nature as the object of another's enjoyment. Sexual desire is at the root of it; and that is why we are ashamed of it.[171]

Then again, the unworldly Prussian professor probably didn't really know what he was talking about, whereas Ayn Rand had, shall we say, a rather colourful love life.

Rand considered herself an Aristotelian. And we can surmise that Aristotle knew a fair bit about this subject because he certainly wrote a lot about it, albeit in a more matter-of-fact style. He made numerous observations (see: COLD FEET), among them that 'One can have intercourse more readily when fasting', and that those 'who are continually on horseback are more inclined for sexual intercourse'. The latter, he explained, was because horsemen are always in motion, hence 'their bodies become open-pored and in a condition that disposes them for sexual intercourse'.[65]

One might expect Epicurus to have written enthusiastically about this pastime. But his reflections on the subject are rather subdued: 'carnal disturbances make you excessively inclined to sexual intercourse. So long as you do not break any laws or disturb any well-established conventions or annoy any of your neighbours or wear down your body or use up your funds you may carry out your own plans as you like,' wrote the supposedly hedonistic philosopher. And, he went on, 'Sex has never benefitted any man.'[134] Who would want to be an Epicurean?

Thomas Aquinas might not have been tempted by carnal pleasures. But he was seemingly tolerant of those who were, for 'there are inclinations which pertain … to natural law, such as sexual relations'.[32] The saintly Italian simply didn't share these proclivities. It is widely reported that his parents were dismayed that young Thomas wanted to join the Church, rather than becoming a knight like his father. In a questionable act of parenting, they locked the adolescent Thomas in a tower and sent naked prostitutes to tempt him. To no avail. In the end, his mother took pity on him, and helped him escape through a window.

SHIPS

'A ship of which a considerable part has been changed by frequent reparations is still considered as the same,' wrote David Hume.[7] Hume, it should be noted, was not the first to think in this way. It was the Greek historian Plutarch (46–119) who first wrote about the debate over whether a much-altered ship remained the same:

> The ship in which Theseus and the young men of Athens returned from Crete had thirty oars, and was preserved by the Athenians ... for they took away the old planks as they rotted away, and put in new ones. This raised a question that divided the philosophers. Some claimed that the ship remained the same, others held that it was a new ship.[172]

It is known as the Ship of Theseus Paradox, and Hume, Hobbes and others drew on this famous thought experiment down the centuries, eventually giving rise, in our own age, to the Sugababes Paradox.

SHIT – see EXCREMENT

SHOES

'Some people have a shoe fetish and there is nothing wrong with that,' the renowned shoe designer Jimmy Choo (b. 1948) is reputed to have said. Notwithstanding the designer's personal profit motive, he was undoubtedly right. Imelda Marcos (b. 1929) the wife of the former Philippines dictator and the mother of the same country's present president, left behind more than 2,700 pairs of shoes when her husband was ousted from power.

We do not know how many pairs of shoes Hannah Arendt owned, but she certainly had a high opinion of footwear. 'What distinguishes the flimsiest pair of shoes from mere consumer goods is that they do not spoil if I do not wear them, that they have an independence of their own, however modest, which enables them to survive even for a considerable time the changing moods of their owner. Used or unused, they will remain in the world for a certain while unless they are wantonly destroyed.'[38]

The American pragmatist philosopher John Dewey (1859–1952) was more interested in the wearing of shoes: 'the man who wears the shoe knows best that it pinches, even if the expert shoemaker is the best judge of how the trouble is remedied'.[173] That expert shoemakers are held in high regard, of course, was nothing new. Plato clearly revered these craftsmen, even to the point that in his dialogues he gives Socrates the line: 'he who does not know what science or knowledge is, has no knowledge of the art or science of making shoes'.[174] By contrast, in Eastern cultures the shoemaker has fared less well in the collective estimation. A famous Chinese proverb goes, 'three smelly leather shoemakers put together can be counted as a Zhuge Liang' – the latter being the greatest statesman during the period of the Three Kingdoms, living approximately in the years 181–234.

SLEEP

René Descartes liked a good lie-in. No wonder the sleepy Frenchman often mused on sleep and dreams in his philosophy. In his *Discourse on Method*, for instance, he wrote that 'asleep we can in the same way imagine ourselves possessed of another body and that we see other stars and another earth, when there is nothing of the kind'.[2] Alas, his employer, Queen Christina of Sweden (1626–89), was an early bird and demanded philosophy lessons at five in the morning. The early starts literally killed the French rationalist, after he caught pneumonia from venturing out in the snowy Swedish dawn.

In his reflections on Morpheus, Descartes followed a popular trend in philosophy from the sixteenth century. Thomas Hobbes would 'often observe the absurdity of dreams, but never dream of the absurdities of [his] waking thoughts', and said that he was 'well satisfied that, being awake, I know that I dream not, though when I dream, I think myself awake'.[25] John Locke was a great fan of sleep, especially among youngsters, 'Nothing is more to be indulged in children than sleep. In this alone they are to be permitted to have their full satisfaction; nothing contributing more to the growth and health of children than sleep.'[70]

Writing around fifty years later, David Hume was of the same mind as Descartes: 'A man sound asleep,' he wrote in *A Treatise of Human Nature*, 'is insensible of time.'[7] Søren Kierkegaard too, another century on, liked to stay in bed, writing with paradoxical playfulness: 'My time I divide as follows: the one half I sleep; the other half I dream. I never dream when I sleep; that would be a shame, because to sleep is the height of genius.'[26]

Plato, on the other hand, had little time for those who preferred to sleep their days away: 'Asleep, man is useless, he may as well be dead.' Unlike his drowsier colleagues, the Athenian philosopher thought 'it a disgrace and unworthy of a gentleman ... if he devotes the whole of any night to sleep'.[48] I write these words in the middle of the night, I hasten to emphasise.

But greater minds than the humble author of this little book also got the memo. Immanuel Kant had his servant wake him up every day at five a.m.

And, based on his indefatigable empirical studies, Aristotle concluded – in the aptly entitled *On Sleep* – that people with small veins, dwarfs and people with large heads sleep a lot. Aristotle surely would not have been surprised that one of Snow White's diminutive cohabitors was named 'Sleepy'. His explanation for dreaming was that it is the result of indigestion.[175]

Hobbes too was interested in the causes of bad dreams. Always unromantic – and true to his mechanistic worldview – the Englishman believed that 'dreams are caused by the distemper of some inward parts of the Body'.[25]

Ethical philosophers have also written about sleep, and what we might call the natural rights of sleepy heads. The Oxford philosopher Philippa Foot (1920–2010) believed it was immoral to photograph a sleeping person. Whether this is a cardinal sin might be debated, but her other sleep-related observation is undeniable: 'In human life it is an Aristotelian necessity (something on which our way of life depends) that if, for instance, a stranger should come on us when we are sleeping, he will not think it all right to kill us.'[176] Without wishing to be disrespectful to one of the greatest female philosophers of all time, this seems to set a rather low bar – both for human decency and for a good night's kip.

Are you still awake? OK, I see… Sweet dreams, then! For, as Nietzsche wrote, 'Blessed are the sleepy ones: for they shall soon nod off.'[67]

SMOKING

In the 1950s, many greengrocers in the Paris markets had a copy of Jean-Paul Sartre's intense theoretical masterpiece *Being and Nothingness*. Published in 1943, the book was a surprising commercial success. Not, perhaps, because the market traders were interested in *the ontology* of phenomenology** – as the subtitle of volume reads. No, more likely it was because the 692-page treatise weighed precisely one kilogram and could be used as a replacement for the copper weights that had been melted down for wartime munitions.

But if the stallholders had flicked through the tome in a quiet moment between customers, they would have read a fair few reflections on smoking. For example, Sartre wrote, 'We everywhere find the same projected unity from the case of artistic creation to that of a cigarette, which is supposed to be better when you roll it yourself.'[177]

According to his partner Simone de Beauvoir, the French philosopher got through two packets of *clopes* a day as well as puffing away on his pipe, and when asked what he considered most important in life, responded, 'everything, living, smoking'.[178]

Finally, Sartre's doctor told him that if he did not stop, he would need to have removed first his legs, then his fingers, and so forth. The existentialist told him that he would think about it, and then declared he would quit on the Monday. Asked by Beauvoir if the thought of smoking his last cigarette filled him with regret, he answered, 'No. To tell you the truth, I find them rather disgusting now.' He never touched tobacco again. For an existentialist, life is to choose. And Sartre did so. Quite something for a man who is often cited for the view that, 'History ... should be nothing else ... than the history of cigarettes.'[178]

Existentialism and smoking seem to go hand in hand. Kierkegaard even compared first love with smoking: 'You so enjoy the moment and gaze into the love, just as the smoker beholds the smoke he exhales.'[33] As much as he liked it, Kierkegaard too was aware that puffing away was not good for you. Reflecting on the best way to get someone to quit smoking, he concluded, 'If I were to discourage a young person from smoking I would just bring him into the smokers' room in Regensen [a famous college for students in Copenhagen where Kierkegaard lived as an undergraduate].'[26] Many philosophers who do not fall into the existentialist category also liked a smoke. When Hannah Arendt attended the Eichmann trial for her book, she avoided the courtroom and stayed in the press room because

she was allowed to smoke her Lucky Strikes – or occasionally a Camel – there. We do not know which brand James Baldwin smoked. But it was a habit he kept up, being rarely pictured without a cigarette on hand, and there are countless references to smoking in his oeuvre. Though, as much as he liked to smoke, he was on some level filled with guilty feelings about the cigarettes in his pocket, as he writes in his 'Letter from a Region in My Mind', published in 1962.[179]

Along with practically every other topic, Bertrand Russell wrote about smoking too. Taking aim at Christianity, as was his wont, the Cambridge philosopher pointed out that tobacco was not prohibited in the Scriptures, though 'St Paul would no doubt have denounced it had he known of it'.[180]

In the nineteenth century, smoking was generally held to be indispensable for thinkers. Victor Hugo (1802–85), author of *The Hunchback of Notre-Dame* and *Les Misérables*, for example, is often cited as claiming that 'tobacco is a plant that converts thoughts into dreams'.[181] This view was echoed over a hundred years later by the Norwegian political philosopher Jon Elster (b. 1940), who would

> organize [my] life around smoking. When things went well, I would reach for a cigarette. When things went badly I would do the same … I always had an excuse for smoking. Smoking became a ritual that served to highlight salient aspects of experience and to impose a structure on what would otherwise have been a confusing morass of events. Smoking provided the commas, semicolons, question marks, exclamation marks, and full stops of experience. It helped me to achieve a feeling of mastery, a feeling that I was in charge of events rather than submitting to them. This craving for cigarettes amounts to a desire for order and control, not for nicotine.[182]

Perhaps so, but cigarettes can be a costly habit, especially if you are a penniless philosopher. Karl Marx knew a thing or two about this. His son-in-law Paul Lafargue recalled that 'Karl Marx was a heavy smoker … "*Das Kapital,*" he said to me once, "will not even pay for the cigars I smoked while writing it," but he was heavier on matches. He so often forgot his pipe or his cigar that he emptied an incredible number of boxes of matches in a short time to relight them.'[183]

Nowadays, we take it for granted that smoking is not permitted on public transport. But this wasn't the case in the mid-nineteenth century, and it annoyed John Stuart Mill. Being something of a contrarian, uniquely for a man of his era he *didn't* like smoking. In 1868, while he was the Member of Parliament for Westminster, he tabled an amendment to the Railway Carriages Bill.

Mill was concerned that the freedom of smokers would have a detrimental effect on non-smokers. This of course would be consistent with his famous harm principle, which says 'that the only purpose for which power can be rightfully exercised over any member of a civilised community, against his will, is to prevent harm to others'.[184]

And Mill saw a need to limit the freedom of smokers, for 'the abuse of smoking had become so great, and the violation of the [rail] companies' by-laws so frequent, that the smoking in trains had become a positive nuisance. Scarcely a railway carriage could be entered in which smoking was not going on, and which was not tainted with stale tobacco'.

But Mill, preferring to operate on consensus, did not advocate a total ban on smoking. Instead, he proposed that 'all Railway Companies shall ... in every passenger train where there are more carriages than one of each class, provide smoking compartments for each class of passengers'.[165] The amendment was passed and for more than a century you were allowed to light up on British trains courtesy of the liberal philosopher. Smoking on board trains was banned in 2005 when both GNER and First Caledonian withdrew smoking accommodation from their services. Mill, we may safely assume, would have been pleased with this decision.

The Nobel Prize-winning French Algerian writer and thinker Albert Camus, another existentialist who was such a big fan of smoking that he even named his cat Cigarette, would have suffered under this regime. Though deeply intelligent and eloquent, Camus – like many of the characters in his fiction, including Meursault, the protagonist of his 1942 novel *The Stranger* – would often prefer to just shut up and smoke a cigarette. I kicked the habit decades ago, but I can see where he is coming from.

SNEEZING

'Ahh, yes, the ecstasy of sneezing': Søren Kierkegaard was not normally one for giving advice on bodily matters, but he was such a big fan of the everyday pleasures of the sneeze that he made an exception in this case and counselled that 'if you really wish to sneeze, then gurgle your nose with water, and if that doesn't work try to tickle your nose', though, he pointed out, this 'would not continue to work'.[116]

Kierkegaard had several beliefs in common with his seventeenth-century predecessor Blaise Pascal, including their agreement on the benevolence of the Almighty, Original Sin and blind obedience to the Deity – and, bizarrely, on sneezing. Like Kierkegaard, the French writer stressed the blissful feeling of sternutation. 'Sneezing absorbs all the functions of the soul,' he wrote.[185]

This enjoyment was not only the preserve of religious bachelors in the modern period. Sneezing was something even the ancient philosophers took pleasure from. Aristotle – normally not given to hyperbole – extolled the feeling associated with this respiratory phenomenon, and pronounced that 'we regard sneezing as divine'. Never one to leave a topic alone, he went on to wonder why 'farting and burping are not regarded as sacred, but that of sneezing is so regarded?' He had an explanation. 'Because this region [the head] is the most sacred, the breath from it is revered.'[66]

So far so good. But certain Anglicans were excessively worried about the consequences of sneezing. Pascal and Kierkegaard – while both hard-line Christian fundamentalists – did not subscribe to this particular form of Christianity. Nor did Bertrand Russell, but he wrote about the dangers of sneezing according to the Church of England. 'Old-fashioned people still say "bless you" when one sneezes, but they have forgotten the reason for this custom. The reason was that people were thought to sneeze out their souls, and before their souls could get back, lurking demons were apt to enter the un-souled. But if you said, "God bless you", the demons were frightened off.'[186]

Perhaps more disturbing is the knowledge that the droplets of a sneeze can travel up to four metres from the offending and possibly germ-laden nostrils. Sadly, though, sneezing is not something we can stop on command, as Wittgenstein observed: 'one produces a sneeze … not out of a voluntary movement'.[42] These days, it's likely we will be more worried about social distancing than about demons entering our souls.

SPORT

We tend to think of philosophers as nerdy types, not jocks or fans of vigorous exercise. So it might come as a surprise that a fair few of them wrote about sport. Aristotle, in a treatise that sadly is lost, wrote about Olympic winners, and Descartes similarly wrote a treatise on the art of fencing. Certainly, these writers took sport seriously. Jean-Jacques Rousseau believed that it was essential for creating social cohesion. In a book written for the Polish government, he advised his clients to make use of sport and spectacular displays. 'Look at Spain, where the bullfights have done much to keep a certain vigour alive in the people', he wrote, before going on to suggest that 'competitions in horsemanship could have much the same effects' as they 'lend themselves to a spectacular display'.[187]

G. W. F. Hegel – half a century after Rousseau – agreed that sport serves a social purpose, and was even more specific: 'wrestling and boxing, running, horse and chariot races, throwing the discus or javelin, and archery … express and form part of the enjoyment of social exhilaration.'[18] Hegel probably didn't have much personal experience as a sportsman. We have no account of him doing push-ups or jogging around the Berlin parks. But his conclusions were not a million miles away from the philosophers who believed that sport had an educational aim. He was a classicist and he had read his Plato.

Like John Rawls (see: BASEBALL), Plato had practical experience with sport (see: WRESTLING) so he knew what he was talking about, and he urged caution. 'The very exercises and tolls which he [an educated person] undergoes are intended to stimulate the spirited element of his nature, and not to increase his strength; he will not, like common athletes, use exercise and regimen to develop his muscles'.

Plato went on to say that 'someone who spends much effort on physical training … by keeping his body in good condition is … filled with resolution and spirit … and become(s) more courageous'.[5]

These words from *The Republic* are all delivered by Socrates. We are apt to think of Socrates as Plato's mouthpiece and believe that the former's utterances were, essentially, inventions by the latter. But it is possible that the real Socrates was speaking on this topic. Socrates, reportedly, was no couch potato and 'took care to exercise his body and kept in good condition'.[56]

Aristotle, Plato's most famous pupil, by contrast, was seemingly not a sporting type – we know that he had very thin legs. But that did not deter him from writing on the subject. Training was suited for young men, but it 'may also hinder growth'.

In fact, too much training as a youngster might not even be useful for the elite sportsmen, for 'amongst the Olympic candidates we can scarce find two or three who have gained a victory both when boys and men: because the necessary exercises they went through when young deprived them of their strength.'[81]

STEALING

Philosophers may not be the most ethical individuals. Not even those who are steeped in moral theories. Kierkegaard, for example, believed that 'what is stolen is most pleasant'.[188] We do not know if the father of existentialism was a shoplifter or a casual pincher of other people's things. But in this tradition of philosophy, there was more than a bit of romanticism for the thief. Thus, Albert Camus remarked approvingly that Sisyphus – the eponymous figure of his famous essay *The Myth of Sisyphus* – was a robber, while Jean-Paul Sartre wrote a book entirely devoted to the writer and convicted thief Jean Genet, entitled *Saint Genet: Actor and Martyr*!

T

TEA

Drinking the infusions of a unique plant from China is a vital part of everyday life in many countries. Naturally, philosophers too have partaken. John Stuart Mill, who worked for the East India Company, was involved in the import of said plant, and appropriately began each day with a cup of tea, though he didn't write much on the subject.

By contrast, Adam Smith wrote a fair bit about the brew. 'Tea,' wrote the philosophy professor turned economist in 1776, 'was a drug very little used in Europe before the middle of the last century.' But Smith was less concerned with the taste of different blends, and more with sales. 'At present the value of the tea annually imported by the English *East India Company*, for the use of their own countrymen, amounts to more than a million and a half a year.' In today's money that would be about £195 million! And this Smith considered to be a conservative estimate as there was 'a great deal more being constantly smuggled into the country from the ports of Holland, from Gottenburgh in Sweden, and from the coast of France too'.[189] Certainly, tea became very popular. George Orwell (1903–50), the author of very British dystopias, naturally also wrote about tea. His conclusion was perhaps controversial.

> Tea – unless one is drinking it in the Russian style – should be drunk without sugar. I know very well that I am in a minority here. But still, how can you call yourself a true tea-lover if you destroy the flavour of your tea by putting sugar in it? It would be equally reasonable to put in pepper or salt. Tea is meant to be bitter, just as beer is meant to be bitter. If you sweeten it, you are no longer tasting the tea, you are merely tasting the sugar; you could make a very similar drink by dissolving sugar in plain hot water.[190]

Fyodor Dostoevsky (1821–81) liked a cuppa too. Though, unsurprisingly, he liked it 'Russian style'. The novelist wrote, 'I say let the world go to hell, but I should always have my tea,' and went on, 'I might foam at the mouth, but … give me a cup of tea with sugar in it, and maybe I should be appeased'.[191]

But, obsessed as the Russian and English novelists were with the hot drink, their not inconsiderable passions fell well short of that of the Chinese poet Lú Tóng (790–835). Active during the Tang Dynasty (618–907), he spent a lifetime writing about this aromatic beverage. 'I am', he wrote, 'in no way interested in immortality, but only in the taste of tea.'[192] Orwell would have disagreed: 'China tea has virtues which are not to be despised nowadays – it is economical, and one can drink it without milk – but there is not much stimulation in it. One does not feel wiser, braver or more optimistic after drinking it'.[190]

TELEPHONE, the

Relative to the 2,400-year span of Western philosophy, the telephone is a recent invention. So, it is perhaps not surprising that it only received attention after the

1930s. Wittgenstein originally trained as a mechanical engineer, but his scientific background may not have been the reason that he pointed out that 'one can transmit talk, but not measles by telephone'.[9] That said, it is hard to dispute as an empirical statement. Other statements about this device are open to question, however. Alexander Graham Bell (1847–1922), who invented the telephone, reportedly said that its great advantage

'over all forms of electrical apparatus consists in the fact that it requires no skill to operate the instrument'. This is an optimistic take. Given how much I – and people of an even older generation – struggle with my smartphone, I am not sure Bell was right.

TENNIS

Thomas Hobbes lived to a grand old age. He was eighty-nine when he died. It is said that he went on long walks and breathed only through his nose for health reasons. But the other reason for his longevity was his habit of playing tennis. This passion even found its way into his philosophy, though he was adamant that there was a difference between political philosophy and mathematics, on the one hand, and racket sports, on the other: 'The skill of making, and maintaining commonwealths, consisteths in certain rules, as doth arithmetic and geometry, not as tennis-play, on practise only.'[25]

Ludwig Wittgenstein never cited Hobbes, nor, as far as we know, did he play tennis. But he wrote about the Englishman's favourite sport, 'In ball games there is winning and losing; but when a child throws his ball at the wall and catches it again, this feature has disappeared. Look at the parts played by skill and luck; and at the difference between skill in chess and skill in tennis.'[10]

John Rawls was more of a baseball man (see: BASEBALL). But he too appreciated tennis, as a sport based on 'the idea that time never runs out'. This means, he went on, 'that there is always time for the losing side to make a comeback'.[12] Perhaps Rawls had been watching the Wimbledon final the year before, in which Björn Borg came back from losing the first set 6 - 1 to John McEnroe and went on to win the match in a five-set classic.

TICKLISHNESS

An element of surprise is essential in many things. 'No one can tickle himself,' wrote Aristotle, 'because one feels the tickling by another person less if one knows beforehand that it is going to take place and more if one does not foresee it.' For that 'which comes unawares tends to deceive'. But why are we ticklish in the first place? Because the ticklish parts are 'regions where the small veins are situated'.[65]

TOILET

'I was taking a dump when I got your note,' begins a letter written by Niccolò Machiavelli. The Florentine political philosopher went on to say that he 'was considering the decay of the world while on the bog'.[193] He was not the only one of the major thinkers to ponder the world from the vantage position of 'the stool', as the smallest room was often called in those days. Martin Luther famously wrote his *Ninety-five Theses* while sat in said place.

Others went even further, and proposed that the entire earth was, well, a shithouse. According to Voltaire,

> Man and woman having been created in the Fourth Heaven, took it into their heads to eat a pancake instead of ambrosia [which] was exhaled through the pores. But after they had eaten pancakes they had to go to the loo. They begged an angel where the bog was.
>
> 'Well, replied the Angel, 'you see that little planet, which is sixty million leagues from here? That is the toilet of the world.

> They went there, this is where they were left, and since then the world has been what it is.[194]

And since then we have been condemned to live not 'in the best of all possible worlds', as his character Dr Pangloss believed, but in what Voltaire considered the celestial equivalent of a toilet.

TOMATO JUICE

The philosopher John Locke famously noted that we take ownership of things when we mix ourselves with a thing that no one previously owned. It is sometimes known as the Lockean Proviso and was formulated in chapter five of his famous *Second Treatise of Government*. So, suppose I produce a bottle of tomato juice and then pour it on the ground, then – indirectly – I mix myself with that piece of soil, and hence I own it. Nearly three hundred years later, this got libertarian philosopher Robert Nozick thinking, 'if you mix your tomato juice in the ocean, [do] you simply lose your juice; [or do you] come to own the ocean [?]'[13]

TROUSERS

In his essay 'On the Custom of Wearing Clothing', Montaigne made a profound – or perhaps silly (take your pick) – remark on the benefits of keeping your pants on. 'If we had been endowed at birth with trousers, I am sure mother nature would have given us a bit of padding on those parts exposed to the elements like she has for the soles of our feet'.[42]

Wittgenstein was more practical and prosaic when he uttered the timeless sentence, 'these trousers don't go with this jacket'. The Austrian philosopher was not, it has to be said, known for his sartorial elegance and always wore the same old tweed jacket. And yet he seemed strangely obsessed with trousers.

In one of his seminars delivered before the Vienna Circle, a philosophical debating society in his hometown in the 1920s, he repeatedly and tellingly – it doesn't seem as if many women were present – drew on this piece of clothing as an example. 'All the people in this room wear trousers. The sentence means that Professor Schlick wears trousers and that Waismann has pants on.' Whether they actually were, we do not know, though it seems highly plausible. But linguistic expression is no guarantee of what goes on in the 'real' world. And that was Wittgenstein's point from a philosophical perspective, for 'how do I know this?' he went on to ask.[74] Characteristically, he did not answer the question he had posed. We can never be sure who wears the trousers – or if indeed they do wear them.

U

URINATION

Diogenes famously urinated in public. What this practical joker of a philosopher meant by it is unclear. Aristotle was characteristically more direct and developed a theory of urination. It goes like this, 'When we stand near a fire we desire to pass urine, and when we stand near water (for example, near a river) we actually piss'.

Aristotle was an observant man, and he believed that he had an explanation. 'It is, he wrote, 'because water in general reminds us of the fluids in our bodies … the neighbourhood of water incites our internal moisture to come out.' And as for the proximity to fire, he had an explanation too: 'it of itself dissolves anything which is solidified in the body, just as the sun melts the snow'.[65]

Lucretius, whose observations were occasionally banal, merely observed that 'little children are lifting up their robes and pissing in public urinals'.[77] Well, with respect, what else should they do? There must have been a deeper meaning. Or maybe the Roman was just taking the piss…

V

VINEYARDS (and WINE)

Arthur Schopenhauer was not much of a drinker. But the famously ascetic German philosopher nevertheless used the vineyard as a metaphor when he pronounced that 'philosophy is related to … arts as wine is to its grapes'.[17]

John Locke took a more direct and empirical interest. 'The older the vineyard, the fewer the grapes,' he observed, before going on, 'but the better the wine.' The Englishman was a bit of a connoisseur. His concern – selfishly, perhaps – was with results, and the production of a good drop.

He duly reported his research and that of others – even when he was himself sceptical. Thus, on his travels to France, he had been told 'that a sheep's horn buried at the root of a vine will make it bear well even in barren ground'. He admitted that he 'had no great faith in it', but added, as a truly open-minded researcher, that he could 'mention it as it might be easily tried'.[195]

He was not alone in writing about the subject. Kierkegaard was not well travelled and never saw a vineyard in his life, yet – confident in his own abilities as he was – he felt qualified to offer advice on the right time to harvest grapes. 'When it is at the point of perfection [it] becomes transparent and clear, while the juice bubbles through its fine veins, as the husk of a fruit breaks when the fruit ripens to all its fullness'.[62]

Unlike Kierkegaard, Hegel did not write much about the subject, but he liked a swig from time to time and sent his wine merchant a request 'for another bottle of Pontac, like the one you previously sent me'.[196]

A lot has been written about the differences between the British empiricists and their speculative colleagues on the Continent. Yet when Locke wrote his treatise *Observations Upon the Growth of Vines and Olives* (1679) he stayed at Château Haut-Brion – then known by the name of the proprietor Monsieur Pontac. Yes, the same man who produced Hegel's favourite drop. So, when it comes to the really important things, the differences were negligible. Let's drink to that!

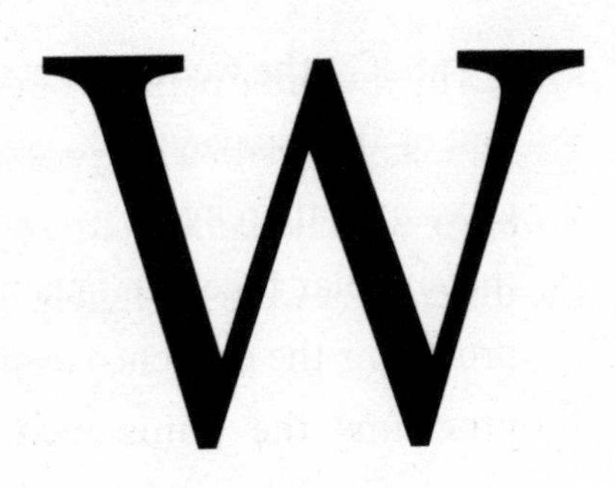

WEDDING PARTY

The average cost of a wedding in Greece is $19,337 (€16,654) in 2022 money.[197] Plato, though as Greek as they come, would not have been impressed. Much as he was an ardent believer in the institution of matrimony (see: MARRIAGE), he was not a fan of excessive nuptials – no big fat Greek weddings for the testy Athenian. 'At the wedding feast,' he decreed, 'neither family should invite more than five friends of both sexes, and the number of relatives and kinsmen from either side should be similarly limited.' The reason for this was pragmatic – indeed social – and not just a sign that the philosopher was a bore, namely that 'no one should incur expenses beyond their means'.[48] Søren Kierkegaard took a different perspective. As a religious thinker, it was hardly surprising that he took a theological – and joyless – view of things.

> What does the wedding ceremony do? It offers, first of all, a survey of the genesis of the human race, and thereby it gives the universal and the singular together. The marriage ceremony proclaims the existence of sin, that the Church proclaims the punishment of sin, that the woman shall bear children with pain and obey her husband. (Whether you do her a service thereby I leave undecided, but I believe you have not grasped the full inner structure of woman, to which also belongs the fact that she is at once more perfect and more imperfect than the man.) … It brings the lovers to a standstill, you say. Not at all, it lets what was already in motion proceed openly.[26]

WINKING

These days you can get in awful trouble if you wink at someone. For Schopenhauer, it seems, refraining from this activity required you to be a god. Greatly inspired by and interested in Indian philosophy and religion as he was, he wrote, 'when the Indian gods appear in human form, they are recognised by not winking'.[17]

WIPING

Montaigne took this universal activity seriously and conducted a detailed study, revealing that the Romans 'wiped their asses with a sponge'. The French essayist relates 'that's why SPONGIA is an uncouth word in Latin. This sponge, by the way, is 'attached to the end of a rod'.[42]

WRESTLING

You might be surprised to learn that perhaps the greatest philosopher of all time was a wrestler – indeed, a victorious contestant in the Isthmian Games. His real name was Aristocles, but he preferred the name his wrestling coach had given him – just as the actor Dwayne Johnson is better known by his WWE wrestling moniker The Rock. Later, once his sporting career was over, this thinker wrote extensively on sport. The name of the renowned wrestler? You guessed it: Plato. The nickname comes from the Greek word for 'the broad-shouldered one'. Contrary to what you might have imagined, Plato did not look like a scrawny nerd: he was a muscular fellow with a physique more like that of Sylvester Stallone than of Arthur Schopenhauer.

So, Plato the pro knew what he was writing about. Though he was pretty old-school, praising 'the legitimate manoeuvres of *regular* wrestling – extricating the neck and hands and sides from entanglement' – and was not a fan of the showier type of this most ancient of the martial arts. The former champion declared that the introduction of 'boxing devices' was 'absolutely useless' and such antics 'don't merit the honour of being described'.

No, Plato insisted that *pálē* – as the most popular sport of the ancient world was called in Greek – 'was practised for the sake of strength and health with a vigorous desire to win and without undignified postures'. He advocated a no-frills, no-nonsense approach to wrestling because this sport was 'extremely useful, and we mustn't neglect it'.[48]

By contrast, recent thinkers have adopted a more esoteric attitude towards the ancient sport of wrestling – though perhaps this merely reflects how aspects of this sport have changed over the centuries. The French structuralist Roland Barthes published an essay on *le catch*, as the sport is known in his language, in his 1957 volume *Mythologies*, in which he placed the emphasis on wrestling as (pseudo-religious) performance. 'What is on display to the public is a great spectacle of suffering, defeat and justice … The wrestler who suffers in a hold … offers an excessive portrayal of suffering; like a primitive Pietà, he exhibits for all to see his face, exaggeratedly contorted by an intolerable affliction'.[198] The contemporary philosopher Lisa Jones takes things further in her analysis of modern pro-wrestling 'All caught up in the kayfabe: understanding and appreciating pro-wrestling', writing that '[pro wrestling] is the fictional representation of sporting conflict. It is perhaps only small children who would take pro-wrestling to be "real", in the same way that they might think Santa Claus is real.'[199]

For John Rawls, so his biographer tells us, wrestling turned out to be all too real and a challenge too far. The philosopher was not good enough to secure a place in the 165-pound weight class, so he tried his luck in the lower division. But this required him to go on a diet, which made him weak. And so, his career as a wrestler came to an end. Just like Plato's. Fortunately, as we have seen, he continued to enjoy baseball (see: BASEBALL).[200]

XENOPHOBIA

Hannah Arendt was a refugee. She had had to run for her life – literally. So, you would *not* expect her to have xenophobic, let alone racist views, such as those harboured by those people who defended Jim Crow laws and racial segregation in the United States. And yet she wrote, 'The right to free association, and therefore to discrimination, has greater validity than the principle of equality.'[201] Yes, it's very sad. But it gets worse.

Great minds, paradoxically, have sometimes been extremely small-minded, and – judging by our standards – overtly xenophobic. Hegel, Kant and Hume, among others, all espoused racist theories of Black inferiority and fixed racialised characteristics.

Some might be tempted to dismiss them altogether and remove them from the curriculum. It is understandable. But it does not solve the problem. Instead, we need to use the tradition against its greatest masters and point out that these ignorant and hurtful ideas go against the main – and positive – traits of the Western philosophical tradition. We need to draw on the established scientific and ethical evidence and methods to refute as well as to condemn.

So, then, why were these thinkers so intolerant? Why did even the greatest minds harbour such prejudices and fears about 'outsiders'? Xenophobia paradoxically only emerged after the Age of Enlightenment. The ancient Greeks took a different attitude. The philosopher Xenophon – who was a tolerant man – proposed a means to help us understand in-group thinking.

> Ethiopians say their gods are flat-nosed and dark,
> Thracians that theirs are blue-eyed and red-haired.
> If oxen and horses and lions had hands and were
> able to draw with their hands and do the same
> things as men, horses would draw the shapes of
> gods to look like horses and oxen to look like

> oxen, and each would make the gods' bodies have the same shape as they themselves had.[202]

Xenophon and Plato had rather distinct views but they both believed in openness to strangers and were very far from being racists. Plato, perhaps reflecting that Zeus is the patron of strangers, wrote, 'The foreigner is not surrounded by friends and companions, and stirs the compassion of the gods.'[48] Another educated man of the Hellenistic era, the Apostle Paul (5–64) took a similar view: 'Be sure to welcome strangers into your home. By doing this, some people have welcomed angels as guests, without even knowing it.'[203]

Y

YAWNING

Those of 'steadfast natures', wrote Plato, 'are apt to yawn and go to sleep over any intellectual toil.'[5] That seems quite accurate. Haven't we all at some stage dozed and yawned over a long meeting or a tricky manuscript? But *why* do we yawn?

The current medical account as proposed by twenty-first-century neurophysiologists stresses that oscitation is triggered when the brain gets too warm; in order to maintain optimal performance, the brain needs to cool down and return to what is called 'thermal homeostasis' – and so a good yawn introduces a flow of cooling oxygen. This is an automatic process that merely follows the laws of physiology. Even Arthur Schopenhauer accepted an earlier version of this theory (see: BATH). Although he believed that we were driven by *will* – he conceded that 'in reflex movements ... such as yawning' this powerful *Urkraft* was not responsible.[17]

Aristotle would have agreed with the cooling-down aspect – as we have seen, he was very attached to his theories of vapours – but he also wanted to go deeper. For Aristotle, in order to understand why something

happens it is not enough merely to look for causes; we must also look for purpose, or what he called 'teleological'* explanations. He wondered, 'Why do men generally themselves yawn when they see others yawn?'[65] To this question science is still yet to find a definitive answer, but it is now acknowledged that contagious yawning has been observed in humans, dogs and non-human primate species.[204] Maybe even scientists need philosophers for inspiration?

Z

ZEALOTS

The original zealots, according to the Jewish historian Josephus (37–100), were members of an ancient Israeli sect which sought to set up a world Jewish theocracy and to kick the Romans out of Palestine around 70 CE.[205] In this they were spectacularly unsuccessful. In reality, these freedom fighters were not doctrinaire – but they lost, and that is not helpful for your reputation in the history books. This probably explains why the word zealot in practical usage has come to signify a fanatic, or true believer.

Philosophers have had different views of extremists. American philosopher George Santayana (1863–1952) said that you were a zealot if you were 'redoubling your effort when you have forgotten your aim'.[206] Even more alarmingly, John Locke concluded that 'zealots hardly have patience to refrain from violence and rapine'.[207]

Kierkegaard, on the other hand, positively endorsed extreme views, as long as they were deeply felt and followed God's diktat. In his famous – and exceptionally disturbing – book *Fear and Trembling* (1843), he argued that there is 'a teleological suspension of the ethical', which translates in plain English to 'the end justifies the means'.[69] The existentialist philosopher even went so far as to justify Abraham's intention to kill Isaac, when God told him, 'Take your son to the land of Moriah and kill [him] as a sacrifice to me.'[208] Of course, God intervened just before Abraham wielded the knife, but this did not matter to Kierkegaard, who as a zealot believed in 'the edifying thought that in front of God we are always in the wrong'.[26]

Zealots are a good thing, believed Kierkegaard, for as he wrote in another eponymous book, 'the purity of the heart is to will one thing'. Or more precisely, 'If a man shall will the good in truth, then he must be willing to do all for the Good' – including slaughtering his own children.[209]

A hundred years earlier, Henry Home, Lord Kames (1695–1782) – a Scottish philosopher, judge and critic – wrote, 'To a zealot every one of his own sect is a saint, while the most upright of a different sect are to him children of perdition'.[210]

POSTSCRIPT

Philosophers have mused a fair bit on endings. Immanuel Kant wrote a famous essay on *The End of All Things* – but he never really got to the point. Roughly half a century later, Søren Kierkegaard penned his famous *Concluding Unscientific Postscript* – an 800-page tome intended to complete his *Philosophical Fragments* – which is itself a short pamphlet of fewer than a hundred pages as it appears in the standard *Collected Works*. Kierkegaard, it seems, had a sense of humour. Or maybe he just needed a copyeditor to tell him where to stop. As a man of independent means, he self-published his books.

Endings are difficult. So are farewells. But in the case of philosophy the issue is – as ever – rather more complex. Other fields of abstract thinking end with conclusions. In mathematics, a proof is finished off with the Latin shorthand *QED* – *quod erat demonstrandum* – 'this has been proved'. Some philosophers have sought to do the same. But to no avail, for philosophy is a discipline or endeavour that only ever ends with more questions. The aim is not to prove something, but to make you think and wonder afresh. So, like all good philosophy, this book too is open-ended, and concludes with an invitation to literally waste your life wondering and pondering, just as some of the greatest minds have done before. Over to you…

GLOSSARY

Yes, this is a book about the smaller things, but philosophers often use words with a specific technical meaning, so – in case you are not already familiar with them – here is a short selection to make understanding easier.

Aesthetics: For philosophers this word is not limited to beauty but to making judgements (which may include subjective ones). For this reason, Kant's famous book *Critique of Judgement* is not just about how we look at art, but how we make judgements in the most general sense of the word.

Analytical (philosophy): In the beginning of the twentieth century, philosophers in Britain began – inspired by Ludwig Wittgenstein – to consider all philosophical problems as problems of language. This tradition, which has been most widespread in the English-speaking world, is known as *analytical* and is often contrasted with *continental** philosophy. One of the most famous thinkers of this tradition was Ludwig Wittgenstein – who, to confuse matters, was Austrian.

Continental (philosophy): A bit of a catch-all portmanteau phrase for all the philosophies in the twentieth century that were not *analytical.* Philosophers in Continental Europe remained interested in the meaning of life (like the existentialists) or in understanding the deeper meaning (including so-called *phenomenologists* who looked for the essence of things). Famous writers in the continental tradition include Jean-Paul Sartre, Martin Heidegger and arguably Hannah Arendt, though she spent most of her life in America.

Empiricism: A doctrine mostly held by British and Irish philosophers (like Locke, Berkeley and Hume), which says that all knowledge is based on experience.

Epistemology: The philosophical subdiscipline concerned with perceiving (or not) the outside world.

It is also called Theory of Knowledge. It comes from the Greek word *epistēmē*, which means scientifically certain knowledge, as opposed to *doxa*, which means opinion or belief.

Ethics: The word, as with so many others in this area, comes from the Greek *ēthikós*, meaning related to one's character. So, in short, the science of being a good person.

Idealism: For Plato, idealism was the belief that all our judgements are comparisons with the ideal forms in heaven. For later philosophers, above all Kant, idealism is the view that all our observations are filtered through our perceptions. The view is summed up in the phrase 'in the eye of the beholder'. Kant also spoke about 'the thing in itself' *(Das Ding an sich)*, which is how things are, independently of our view of them.

Logic: Normal people who have not studied philosophy tend to use the word 'logical' to mean rational or reasonable. For philosophers, it is something different. Logic is about pure form. For example, for a logician the sentences, 'If I am hungry, then there is food in the fridge. I am hungry. Hence there is food in the fridge' are logically true, because they are formalised as: If P then Q; P, therefore Q. Even if, in reality, you are still waiting hungrily for the Waitrose delivery. This is obviously a bit silly. But that's how it is!

Metaphysics: For philosophers this refers to statements about the nature of things. It comes from the Greek for 'after' (*meta*) and 'physics'. It need not – though it can – have anything to do with supernatural notions or entities like God or the soul. So, in essence, this term describes what the world is like in a deeper sense and relates to high-level notions of 'cause', 'effect', 'possibility' and 'being' (see also 'ontology'). So, for a philosopher, it is a metaphysical statement to say that you are holding a book in your hands.

Ontology: 'To be or not to be', that was the question for Shakespeare's Hamlet. When the Danish Prince was pondering this, he was – probably without knowing it – engaged in ontology. This is philosopher speak for 'the study of being', or what it means in a deeper sense to exist. Yes, the Greeks had a word for it. The word *ontos* means 'that which is'.

Phenomenology: A doctrine in continental philosophy that says that philosophy should study things as they seem to us. The Greek word *phainómenon* translates as 'that which appears'.

This is how the philosopher Hegel used the word in his (fiendishly difficult) book *The Phenomenology of the Spirit*. In the twentieth century, Edmund Husserl (1859–1938) described 'the phenomenon' as the intuitive experience of things.

Post-Structuralism: Sometimes known as postmodernism, this school of thought was largely a reaction to *Structuralism*. Post-structuralists, like Jean Baudrillard (1929–2007), questioned the grand narraives and argued for a more or less radical way of thinking that challenged the ideas of structuralism, but also, more widely, the rational ideas of the Enlightenment (that had emanated from thinkers like Descartes). One of the most famous books of the school is Baudrillard's *La Guerre du Golfe n'a pas eu lieu* (1991), which translates as 'The Gulf War Did Not Take Place'.

Rationalism: A view mostly held by Continental European philosophers (like Descartes, Spinoza and Leibniz), which says that knowledge comes from our mind, and not from experience. For this reason, Descartes could start his ponderings with, 'I think', before he concluded, 'therefore I am'. Everything he did thereafter was all in the mind.

Realism: The philosophical view that the external world exists independently of our perceptions of it.

Structuralism: In the 1960s, French literary critics, philosophers, anthropologists and other writers in the humanities began to look for ways in which their study could become more scientific. The French anthropologist Claude Lévi-Strauss (1908–2009) was the first scholar to look for these structures in his studies of tribes. Later, the French Marxist Louis Althusser

(1918–90) argued in his book *For Marx* (1965) that Marxism was a scientific system and that students had better avoid the early, more poetic Marx.

Teleological: The Greek word *telos* means goal, and the term describes anything that has a distinct (often forward) aim or direction, typically an action.

ENDNOTES

1 Descartes, René. Letter to the Marquess of Newcastle, 23rd November 1646.

2 Descartes, René. (1987). *Discours de la méthode*. Paris: Vrin.

3 Berkeley, George. (1710). *A treatise concerning the principles of human knowledge*. Dublin: RS Bear.

4 Avicenna. (2013). *Kitab al-Ta'līqāt*. S. H. Mousavian (ed.). Tehran: Iranian Institute of Philosophy.

5 Plato. (1930). *The Republic*. London: Loeb.

6 Aristotle. (1991). *History of Animals*, Vol. 3. Cambridge, MA: Harvard University Press.

7 Hume, David. (1964). *A Treatise of Human Nature*. Oxford: Clarendon Press.

8 Kant, Immanuel. (2016). *Grundlegung zur Metaphysik der Sitten*. Dieter Schönecker (ed.). Hamburg: Felix Meiner.

9 Wittgenstein, Ludwig. (1967). *Zettel*. Frankfurt aM: Suhrkamp.

10 Wittgenstein, Ludwig. (2003). *Philosophische Untersuchungen*. Frankfurt aM: Suhrkamp.

11 Rawls, John. (1971). *A Theory of Justice*. Oxford: Oxford University Press.

12 Rawls, John. Letter to Owen Fiss, 18th April 1981. https://www.bostonreview.net/articles/rawls-the-best-of-all-games/ Accessed 29th July 2023.

13 Nozick, Robert. (1974). *Anarchy, State, and Utopia*. Oxford: Blackwell.

14 Beauvoir, Simone de. 'My Clothes and I'. Interview in *Observer*, 20th March 1960.
15 https://www.mirashowers.co.uk/blog/trends/revealed-what-brits-are-really-getting-up-to-in-the-bathroom-1/ Accessed 22nd January 2023.
16 https://www.mirashowers.co.uk/blog/trends/10-of-the-world-s-greatest-achievements-to-come-out-of-the-bathroom/ and https://www.pmmag.com/articles/96968-hansgrohe-study-the-brightest-ideas-begin-in-the-shower/ Accessed 12th June 2023.
17 Schopenhauer, Arthur. (2009). *Die Welt als Wille und Vorstellung: Vollständige Ausgabe nach der dritten, verbesserten und beträchtlich vermehrten Auflage von 1859.* Berlin: Anaconda.
18 Hegel, G. W. F. (1986). *Vorlesungen über die Geschichte der Philosophie*. Frankfurt aM: Suhrkamp.
19 Epictetus. (1928). *Discourses*, Books 3–4. *The Encheiridion*. London: Loeb.
20 Mary McCarthy, quoted in 'Hannah Arendt's Female Friends', *Los Angeles Review of Books*, 12th November 2013.
21 Nietzsche, Friedrich. (1889). *Götzen-Dämmerung, oder, Wie man mit dem Hammer philosophiert*. Berlin: DeGruyter.
22 'Scots "drink 120 pints of beer a year more than the English"', *Daily Telegraph*, 21st July 2010.
23 Locke, John. Quoted in Peter King. (1958). *The Life of John Locke*. London: Henry Bohn, 15.
24 Bacon, Francis. (1878). *Novum organum*. Oxford: Clarendon Press.
25 Hobbes, Thomas. (2009). *Leviathan*. Oxford: Oxford University Press.
26 Kierkegaard, Søren. (1843). *Enten-Eller.* Copenhagen: Hans Reizel.
27 Seeley, Thomas. (2010). *Honeybee Democracy.* Princeton, NJ: Princeton University Press. Illustrated edition.

28 Descartes, René. (1985). *Philosophical Writings of Descartes*, Vol. II. Cambridge: Cambridge University Press.

29 Epicurus. Letter to Menoikeus, translated by Peter Saint-Andre, https://monadnock.net/epicurus/letter.html/ Accessed 28th March 2023.

30 Epicurus. Letter to Menoikeus, translated by Robert Drew Hicks, http://classics.mit.edu/Epicurusmenoec.html/ Accessed 14th April 2023.

31 Wollstonecraft, Mary. (2014). *A Vindication of the Rights of Woman*. New Haven, CT: Yale University Press.

32 Aquinas, Thomas. (2006). *Summa Theologiae*. Cambridge: Cambridge University Press.

33 Hume, David. In David Fate Norton, Jacqueline Taylor (eds.). (1993). *The Cambridge Companion to David Hume*. Cambridge: Cambridge University Press.

34 Hegel, G. W. F. (1986). *Vorlesungen über die Ästhetik*. Frankfurt aM: Suhrkamp.

35 Heidegger, Martin, (2022). *Bauen Wohnen Denken: Vorträge und Aufsätze*. Hamburg: Klett-Cotta.

36 Wittgenstein, Ludwig. (2013). *Kulturen und Werte*. Berlin: DeGruyter.

37 Russell, Bertrand. (1974). *Why I am Not a Christian and Other Essays on Religion and Related Subjects*. London: Routledge and Kegan Paul.

38 Arendt, Hannah. (1956). *The Human Condition*. New York: Harcourt.

39 Derrida, Jacques. Quoted in Mathieu Luca. 'The Animal That Therefore I Am: Jacques Derrida and His Cat'. https://mathieu-laca.com/jacques-derrida-cat/ Accessed 12th June 2023

40 Temple, Emily. 'This is just a reminder that Albert Camus named his cat Cigarette, because of course he did'. (2022.) Lit Hub. https://lithub.com/this-is-just-a-reminder-that-albert-camus-named-his-cat-cigarette-because-of-course-he-did/ Accessed 12th June 2023

41 Schrödinger, Edwin. (1935). *'Die gegenwärtige Situation*

in der Quantenmechanik'. Naturwissenschaften, Vol. 23, 807–812.
42 Montaigne, Michel de. (2019). *Essais*. Paris: Hachette.
43 Leibniz, G. W. Letter to Johann Bernoulli, 17th December 1698. http://philosophyfaculty.ucsd.edu/faculty/rutherford/Leibniz/Couturatchapters/Note15.pdf/ Accessed 17th June 2023.
44 Epicurus. *Fragments*. In Eugene O'Connor (ed. and trans.). (1993). *The Essential Epicurus*. Amherst, NY: Prometheus Books.
45 Locke, John. (1996). *Of the Conduct of the Understanding*. Indianapolis, IN: Hackett.
46 Stevenson, Robert Louis. (2012). *Treasure Island*. London: Penguin.
47 Keynes, John Maynard. Quoted in *New York Times*, 5th November 2009.
48 Plato. (1989). *Laws*, Vols. I-II. Cambridge, MA: Loeb.
49 Wollstonecraft, Mary. (1985). *Works*, Vol. VII. London: Routledge.
50 Wollstonecraft, Mary. (1985). *Letters*. In *Works*, Vol. VI. London: Routledge.
51 Baggini, Julian. Quoted in 'The Virtues of the Table: How to Eat and Think', *Guardian*, 12th January 2014.
52 Gaulle, Charles de. (2021). *The New Yale Book of Quotations*. New Haven, CT: Yale University Press, 203.
53 Spinoza, Benedict de. (1996). *Ethics*. London: Penguin.
54 *Bulletin Cartésien*, XXXI, Centre d'Études Cartésiennes, 2003, 151–183.
55 Shorto, Russell. (2008). *Descartes' Bones: A Skeletal History of the Conflict Between Faith and Reason*. New York: Random House, 18.
56 Diogenes Laërtius. (1925). *Lives of Eminent Philosophers*, Vol. II: Books 6-10. Translated by R. D. Hicks. Loeb Classical Library 185. Cambridge, MA: Harvard University Press.
57 Russell, Bertrand. (2009). *Mortals and Others*. London: Routledge.

58 Quincey, Thomas De. (2018). *The Last Days of Immanuel Kant.* London: HardPress.
59 Murdoch, Iris. (2001). *The Sea, The Sea.* London: Vintage.
60 Anscombe, G. E. M. Quoted in Michael Freeman (ed.). (2001). *Ethics and Medical Decision-Making.* London: Routledge.
61 Garff, Joakim. (2005). *Kierkegaard: A Biography.* Princeton, NJ: Princeton University Press, 288.
62 Kierkegaard, Søren. (1845). *Gentagelsen.* Copenhagen: Hans Reizel.
63 Voltaire, in *Mercure de France*, 4th October 1783.
64 Beauvoir, Simone de. (1954). *Les Mandarins.* Paris: Gallimard.
65 Aristotle. (2011). *Problems.* Cambridge, MA: Loeb.
66 Aristotle. (2011). *Parts of Animals.* Cambridge, MA: Loeb.
67 Nietzsche, Friedrich. (1883). *Thus Sprach Zarathustra.* Berlin: Alfred Kröner.
68 Kierkegaard, Søren. (1961). *Filosofiske Smugler.* Copenhagen: Gyldendal.
69 Kierkegaard, Søren. (1960). *Frygt og Bæven. Samlede Værker Fem.* Copenhagen: Gyldendal.
70 Locke, John. (1996). *Some Thoughts Concerning Education.* Indianapolis, IN: Hackett.
71 al-Farabi. *Summary of Plato's Laws* in Charles E. Butterworth (ed. and trans.). (2015). *The Political Writings,* Vol. II. Ithaca, NY: Cornell University Press.
72 Arendt, Hannah. (2000). *Rahel Varnhagen: The Life of a Jewess.* Baltimore, MD: Johns Hopkins University Press.
73 Quoted in Alix Kates Shulman. 'Dances with Feminists'. *Women's Review of Books*, Vol. IX, No. 3, December 1991.
74 Wittgenstein, Ludwig. Quoted in Friedrich Waismann and B. F. McGuinness (eds.) (1967). *Wittgenstein und der Wiener Kreis.* Frankfurt aM: Suhrkamp.
75 Kierkegaard, Søren. (1843). *Den Ullykkeligste.* Copenhagen: Hans Reizel.

76 Diogenes Laërtius. https://penelope.uchicago.edu/~grout/encyclopaedia_romana/greece/hetairai/diogenes.html Accessed 18th July 2023.

77 Lucretius. (1924). *On the Nature of Things*. London: Loeb.

78 Marx, Heinrich. Quoted in David McLellan. (2004). *Karl Marx: A Biography*. London: Macmillan, 26.

79 Mill, John Stuart. Diary entry for 10th January 1854. In J. M. Robson (ed.). (2006). *The Collected Works of John Stuart Mill, Volume XXVII - Journals and Debating Speeches Part II*. Toronto: Toronto University Press.

80 Russell, Bertrand. (1971). *In Praise of Being Idle*. London: Routledge and Kegan Paul.

81 Aristotle. (1988). *Politics*. Cambridge: Cambridge University Press.

82 Voltaire. Letter to the Marquis of Jaucourt, 1770.

83 Soros, George. 'Soros: General Theory of Reflexivity', *Financial Times*, 26th September 2009.

84 Anscombe, G. E. M. Quoted in her *Guardian* obituary, 11th January 2001.

85 Plato. (1988). *Parmenides*. London: Loeb.

86 Aristotle. (1891). *Constitution of Athens*. London: Seeley & Co. https://oll.libertyfund.org/title/dymes-constitution-of-athens Accessed 29th July 2023.

87 Luther, Martin. Quoted in Danielle Mead Skjelver. 'German Hercules: The Impact of Scatology on the Definition of Martin Luther as a Man 1483–1546'. *Pittsburgh Undergraduate Review*, Vol. 14, No. 1, 2009, 15.

88 Wittgenstein, Ludwig. Quoted in David Edmonds and John Eidinow. 'Wittgenstein's Poker'. *Guardian*, 21st November 2001.

89 Tomlin, J., C. Lowis and N. W. Read. 'Investigation of normal flatus production in healthy volunteers'. *Gut*, 32(6), 1991, 665–9.

90 Aristophanes. (2000). *The Birds*. Cambridge, MA: Loeb.

91 Aristophanes. (2001). *The Clouds*. Cambridge, MA: Loeb.

92 Hippocrates of Kos. (2012). *Regimen in Acute Diseases.* Cambridge, MA: Loeb.
93 Swift, Jonathan. (2017). *The Benefit of Farting Explained.* Richmond: Alma Books.
94 Hadīth Muhammad ibn 'Abd Allāh al-Ansārī 42.
95 Hume, David. Letter to Dr George Cheyne. In *The Cambridge Companion to David Hume*, 519.
96 Weil, Simone. (2019). *L'enracinement: Prélude à une déclaration des devoirs envers l'être humain.* Paris: Passarino.
97 Augustine. (1957). *The City of God.* London: Loeb.
98 Wittgenstein, Ludwig. (1961). *Notebooks 1914–1916.* Oxford: Blackwell.
99 Satre, Jean-Paul. Quoted in 'L'autre planète foot'. *Le Monde*, 31st May 2002.
100 On Heidegger and Beckenbauer, see Rüdiger Safranski. (1998). *Martin Heidegger – Between Good and Evil.* Cambridge, MA: Harvard University Press, 428.
101 Wenger, Arsène. Quoted in 'Premiership anarchy could drive Arsène away'. *Daily Mail*, 10th November 2010.
102 Mourinho, José. Quoted in 'Mourinho says he is one of the great managers – and quotes Hegel to prove it'. *Guardian*, 31st August 2018.
103 Interview with Bill Shankly by Shelley Rohde on *Live at Two*, Granada TV, 20th May 1981. https://www.youtube.com/watch?v=Vu0P4mI73VY Accessed 18th July 2023.
104 Derrida, Jacques. Cited in Michael Dillon 'Derrida', in T. Carver, J. Martin (eds.). (2005). *Palgrave Advances in Continental Political Thought.* London: Palgrave, 260.
105 Voltaire. (2015). *Candide ou l'Optimisme.* Paris: Gallimard.
106 Rubinger, C. (1994). 'Some Gardens in the French Eighteenth-Century Novel'. *Dalhousie French Studies*, 85–95.
107 Cicero. (2016). *How to Win an Argument: An Ancient Guide to the Art of Persuasion.* Princeton, NJ: Princeton University Press.

108 Bacon, Francis. *Of Gardens*. https://arlene1027.wordpress.com/francis-bacon-wrote-that-a-garden-is-the-purest-of-human-pleasures-it-is-the-greatest-refreshment-to-the-spirits-of-man-without-which-buildings-and-palaces-are-but-gross-handiworks-how-right-he/ Accessed 17th June 2023.
109 More, Thomas. (2012). *Utopia*. London: Penguin.
110 Milton, John. (2001). *Paradise Lost*. London: Penguin.
111 Confucius. (1979). *Analects*. London: Penguin.
112 Luke 7:34.
113 al-Farabi. 'Political Regime' in Butterworth, *The Political Writings*, Vol. II.
114 Kant, Immanuel. (1992). *Grundlegung zur Metaphysik der Moral*. Frankfurt aM: Suhrkamp.
115 Plato. (1989). *Symposium*. Cambridge, MA: Loeb.
116 Kierkegaard, Søren. (1962). *Samlede Papirer*. Copenhagen: Gyldendal.
117 Lord Byron. Letter to Thomas Moore, 31st October 1815.
118 Thomas, Emily. (2020). *The Meaning of Travel*. Oxford: Oxford University Press.
119 Popper, Karl. (1963). *Conjectures and Refutations*. London: Routledge and Kegan Paul.
120 Andersen, Hans Christian. (1870). *Mit Livs Eventyr*. Copenhagen: Gyldendal.
121 Shakespeare, William. *Henry VI*, Part 3, Act 3, Scene 2.
122 Machiavelli, Niccolò. Letter to Luigi Guicciardini, 9th December 1509. https://www.scribd.com/document/520228264/Machiavelli-to-Luigi-in-Mantua-1509/ Accessed 17th June 2023.
123 Rousseau, Jean-Jacques. Quoted in Leo Damrosch. (2005). *Jean-Jacques Rousseau: Restless Genius*. Boston, MA: Houghton Mifflin Harcourt, 178.
124 Plato. (1989). *Cratylus*. Cambridge, MA: Loeb.
125 Antisthenes. Quoted in Simplicius. (2014). *On Aristotle Categories 1–4*. London: Bloomsbury Academic.

126 Hume, David. (1990). *Essays, Literary, Moral, and Political.* Indianapolis, IN: Liberty Fund.

127 Julius Caesar. (2019). *Caesar's Gallic War.* New York: Forgotten Books.

128 Kierkegaard, Søren. (1854). *Øjeblikket.* Copenhagen: Gyldendal.

129 Popper, Karl. Quoted in *Intellectus*, Vol. 23, July 1992. http://www.tkpw.net/hk-ies/n23a/ Accessed 17th June 2023.

130 Epicurus cited in Diogenes Laërtius, *Lives of Eminent Philosophers*, 108.

131 Descartes, René. Letter to Christiaan Huygens. 7th December 1640. Quoted in Christiane Vilain. (1998). '*Descartes, correspondant scientifique de Constantyn Huygens*'. *Revue d'histoire des sciences Année,* 373 - 380, 378.

132 Freud, Sigmund. (2021). *Der Witz und seine Beziehung zum Unbewußten: Sigmund-Freud.* Berlin: Neopubli.

133 Arendt, Hannah. Quoted in *Los Angeles Review of Books*, 13th August 2016.

134 Epicurus. *Vatican Aphorisms.* https://epicurus.net/en/vatican.html/ Accessed 17th June 2023.

135 Bergson, Henri. (2013). *Le Rire.* Paris: Flammarion.

136 Arendt, Hannah. (1978). *The Life of the Mind.* New York: Harcourt.

137 Earl of Shaftesbury. (1709). *Sensus Communis: An Essay on the Freedom of Wit and Humour.* https://www.earlymoderntexts.com/assets/pdfs/shaftesbury1709a_1.pdf/ Accessed 25th June 2023.

138 Kant, Immanuel. (1990). *Kritik der Urteilskraft.* Hamburg: Felix Meiner.

139 Lafargue, Paul. (2015). *Le droit à la paresse.* Paris: Shs Editions.

140 Lessing, G. E. 'Lob der Faulheit'. https://www.lieder.net/lieder/get_text.html?TextId=10167/ Accessed 17th June 2023.

141 Haydn, Joseph. 'Lob der Faulheit', song for voice and keyboard. H. 26a/22.
142 Kierkegaard, Søren. (1845). *Liljerne på Marken og Fuglene i Himlen*. Copenhagen: Gyldendal.
143 Roland Barthes. Quoted in https://foucart.net/2010/07/01/lecoute-selon-roland-barthes/ Accessed 17th June 2023.
144 Augustine. (2005). *De Civitate Dei*. New York: Aris and Phillips Classical Texts.
145 Marsilius of Padua. (1932). *Defensor Pacis*, Part III, ch. ii. In Goldet. *Monarchia Sancti Romani Imperii*. https://img1.wsimg.com/blobby/go/4cb1e8a7-0f1a-4c3a-ae4d-65ac09f78b80/downloads/fujuboji.pdf/ Accessed 17th June 2023.
146 Mill, John Stuart. Diary entry for 9th January 1854. *The Collected Works of John Stuart Mill, Volume XXVII – Journals and Debating Speeches Part II*.
147 Arendt, Hannah–Martin Heidegger. (2002). *Briefe 1925–1975*. Frankfurt aM: Vittorio Klosterman.
148 Arendt, Hannah. (1996). *Love and Saint Augustine*. Chicago: University of Chicago Press.
149 Ortega y Gasset, José. (1967). *On Love*. London: Jonathan Cape.
150 Hegel, G. W. F. (2021). *Hegel, Grundlinien der Philosophie des Rechts oder Naturrecht und Staatswissenschaft im Grundrisse*. Hamburg: Felix Meiner.
151 Marx, Karl. (2016). *Das Kapital. Erster Band. Buch I: Der Produktionsprozess des Kapitals*. Werke 23. Berlin: Dietz.
152 Beauvoir, Simone de. (1949). *Le deuxième sexe*. Paris: Gallimard.
153 Andersen, Hans Christian. (1990). *Kejserens Nye Klæder*. Copenhagen: Gyldendal.
154 Galilei, Galileo. *The Assayer*. Quoted from https://web.stanford.edu/~jsabol/certainty/readings/Galileo-Assayer.pdf/ Accessed 17th June 2023.
155 Epicurus. Letter to Herodotus. Quoted from https://www.attalus.org/old/diogenes10b.html/ Accessed 17th June 2023.

156 Martial. XI, lxviii, 20. Quoted from https://www.tertullian.org/fathers/martial_epigrams_book11.htm/ Accessed 17th June 2023.
157 Plato. (1989). *Timaeus*. Cambridge, MA: Loeb.
158 Aristotle. (1989). *Generation of Animals*. Cambridge, MA: Loeb.
159 Lord Byron. (2018). *Manfred*, Act 1, Scene 1. London: Wilder Publications.
160 Rousseau, Jean-Jacques. (2014). *Émile ou De l'éducation de Jean-Jacques Rousseau (Fiche de lecture): Résumé complet et analyse détaillée de l'oeuvre*. Paris: le Petit Littéraire.
161 Freud, Sigmund. (2010). *'Der Dichter und das Phantasieren': Schriften zur Kunst und Kultur*. Leipzig: Reclam.
162 Augustine. (1933). *Confessions*. London: Loeb.
163 Matthew 18:3.
164 Marc A. Fajer. (1992). 'Can Two Real Men Eat Quiche Together? – Storytelling, Gender-Role Stereotypes, and Legal Protection for Lesbians and Gay Men'. *University of Miami Law Review*, 511.
165 Mill, John Stuart. (2006). *Public and Parliamentary Speeches*. Toronto: Toronto University Press.
166 Pascal, Blaise. Quoted in 'This column will change your life'. *Guardian*, 19th July 2014.
167 Catullus. *A Warning: to Aurelius*. https://allpoetry.com/A-Warning:-to-Aurelius Accessed 29th July 2023.
168 Laozi. Cited in Bertrand Russell. (2009). *Unpopular Essays*. London: Routledge.
169 Plato. (1888). *The Republic of Plato*. Translated by B. Jowett. London: Oxford University Press, 390.
170 Rand, Ayn. (1991). *The Voice of Reason*. Harmondsworth: Penguin.
171 Kant, Immanuel. (2021). *Kants Metaphysik Der Sitten: Der Zusammenhang Von Rechts- Und Tugendlehre*. Berlin: DeGruyter.
172 Plutarch. (1914). *The Life of Theseus*. London: Loeb.

173 Dewey, John. (2001). *Political Writings.* Indianapolis, IN: Hackett.
174 Plato. (1921). *Theaetetus. Sophist.* Translated by Harold North Fowler. Loeb Classical Library 123. Cambridge, MA: Harvard University Press.
175 Aristotle. (1911). *De Somno.* London: Loeb.
176 Foot, Philippa. (2003). *Natural Goodness.* Oxford: Clarendon Press.
177 Sartre, Jean-Paul. (1943). *L'Être et le Néant. Essai D'Ontologie Phénoménologique.* Paris: Gallimard.
178 Sartre, Jean-Paul. Quoted in Richard Klein. (1993). *Cigarettes Are Sublime.* Durham, NC: Duke University Press.
179 Baldwin, James. 'Letter from a Region in My Mind'. *New Yorker*, 9th November 1962.
180 Russell, Bertrand. (2009). *Basic Writings of Bertrand Russell.* London: Routledge.
181 Hugo, Victor. Quoted in https://geudensherman.wordpress.com/2019/06/16/victor-hugo-contre-le-tabac/ Accessed 19th July 2023.
182 Elster, Jon. (1999). *Strong Feelings, Emotion, Addiction, and Human Behavior.* Boston, MA: MIT Press.
183 Lafargue, Paul. (1890). *Reminiscences of Marx.* Quoted from https://www.marxists.org/archive/lafargue/1890/xx/marx.htm/ Accessed 18th Jun 2023.
184 Mill, John Stuart. (1989). *On Liberty.* Cambridge: Cambridge University Press.
185 Pascal, Blaise. (2008). *Pensées.* Paris: Flammarion.
186 Russell, Bertrand. *Unpopular Essays.*
187 Rousseau, Jean-Jacques. (1964). *Écrits Politiques.* Eds. Bernard Gagnebin and Marcel Raymond. Paris: Gallimard.
188 Kierkegaard, Søren. (1967). *Johannes Climacus.* Copenhagen: Gyldendal.
189 Smith, Adam. (1976). *An Inquiry into the Nature and Causes of the Wealth of Nations.* Indianapolis, IN: Liberty Fund.

190 Orwell, George. *Evening Standard*, 12th January 1946.
191 Dostoevsky, Fyodor. (1994). *Notes from the Underground*. London: Vintage.
192 Lú Tóng. Quoted in Steven D. Owyoung. (2011). 'Lu T'ung and the Song of Tea', Kyoto Journal. https://www.kyotojournal.org/fiction-poetry/lu-t%E2%80%99ung-and-the-song-of-tea/ Accessed 19th July 2023.
193 Machiavelli, Niccolò. Letter to Francesco Guicciardini, 17th May 1521. http://legalhistorysources.com/ChurchHistory220/Lecture13/MachiavelliFranceso.html/ Accessed 18th June 2023.
194 Voltaire. (2008). *Dictionnaire philosophique*. Paris: Gallimard.
195 Locke, John. (2010). *Observations Upon the Growth and Culture of Vines and Olives*. Farmington Hills, MI: Gale ECCO.
196 Hegel, G. W. F. Letter to Gebrüder Ramann, 12th October 1802. Quoted from https://www.christies.com/en/lot/lot-5447773/ Accessed 18th June 2023.
197 This is half of the average cost of a wedding held in the UK, even when purchasing power differences are taken into account.
198 Barthes, Roland. (2011). *Mythologies*. Paris: Seuil.
199 Jones, Lisa. (2019). 'All caught up in the kayfabe: understanding and appreciating pro-wrestling'. *Journal of the Philosophy of Sport*, *46*(2), 276–291.
200 Pogge, Thomas. (2007). *John Rawls: His Life and Theory of Justice*. New York: Oxford University Press USA, 10.
201 Arendt, Hannah. (1959). 'Reflections on Little Rock'. *Dissent Magazine*, https://www.dissentmagazine.org/article/reflections-on-little-rock/ Accessed 18th June 2023.
202 Xenophon. Cited in Clement, *Miscellanies V*. London: Routledge, 110.
203 Hebrews 13:2.
204 Provine, R. R. (1986). 'Yawning as a stereotyped action pattern and releasing stimulus'. *Ethology*, *72*(2), 109–122.

205 Josephus, Flavius. (1998). *Antiquities of the Jews.* Cambridge, MA: Loeb.
206 Santayana, George. (2011). *The Life of Reason: Reason in Common Sense.* Vol. VII, Book 1. Cambridge, MA: MIT Press.
207 Locke, John. (1988). *Letter Concerning Toleration.* Indianapolis, IN: Hackett.
208 Genesis 22:2.
209 Kierkegaard, Søren. (1961). *Hjertets Renhed er at Ville Et.* Copenhagen: Gyldendal.
210 Lord Kames. (2001). *Elements of Criticism.* London: Adamant Media Corporation.